easy
italian

photography by Peter Cassidy

quadrille

This edition first published in 2005 by **Quadrille Publishing Limited**
Alhambra House, 27-31 Charing Cross Road, London WC2H 0LS

Editorial director Jane O'Shea
Creative director Helen Lewis
Managing editor Janet Illsley
Art direction Vanessa Courtier
Design Ros Holder and Sue Storey
Photographer Peter Cassidy
Food stylist Linda Tubby
Props stylist Jane Campsie
Editor Susan Fleming
Production Ruth Deary

Text © 2003 Ursula Ferrigno **Photography** © 2003 Peter Cassidy
Design and layout © 2005 Quadrille Publishing Limited

Reprinted in 2007
10 9 8 7 6 5 4 3 2

Originally published exclusively for J Sainsbury plc.

Cataloguing in Publication Data: a catalogue record for this book is available
from the British Library.

ISBN: 978 184400 212 2

Printed in China

Cookery notes
All spoon measures are level: 1 tsp = 5ml spoon; 1 tbsp = 15ml spoon.
Use fresh herbs and freshly ground black pepper unless otherwise suggested.
Free-range eggs are recommended and large eggs should be used except
where a different size is specified. Recipes with raw or lightly cooked eggs
should be avoided by anyone who is pregnant or in a vulnerable health group.

Contents

Introduction

Italian cuisine is arguably the most delectable, the most influential, in short, the best loved cuisine in the world. Italian recipes have made an enormous difference to the way we cook. Quite apart from the perpetual presence of the best known Italian exports in our lives – pasta, pizza and Parmesan, to name a few – so many things we eat have their roots in Italian cuisine. The way we assemble a salad, prepare a pasta dish, or grill a piece of fish or meat, indicate how strong these influences are. When the preparation of food is at its simplest and best, it often owes a debt to the Italian kitchen.

The fact that Italian cooking is so simple, virtually guarantees success every time you start to work in the kitchen. I believe that the essence of good food lies in simplicity. I also endorse the popular Italian saying 'piu se spenne peggio se magna' (the more you spend the less well you eat). Italian food is not expensive or difficult: it is all about good basic ingredients, simply prepared and lovingly cooked, to produce a meal that hasn't taken all day to create.

There are no difficult techniques to master in Italian cooking, although pasta-making and bread-making are more time-consuming and a little more complex. Both lie at the heart of the Italian eating experience and once you have learnt the simple rules, you will be able to create fabulous breads, pizzas and homemade pasta. Because Italian cooking is essentially easy, it inspires confidence in the kitchen. And a confident cook, working with good ingredients, is a successful cook.

All the recipes here are easily achievable. All are authentically Italian, and even those I've invented myself have their roots firmly in Italian tradition. Having been brought up in Italy, and having learnt the huge respect accorded to food and eating at first hand, my recipes could be nothing other than traditional. The book is roughly arranged as an Italian meal would be, beginning with easy antipasti or starters, soups and breads. The course that follows – pasta, polenta or risotto – is also simple. Neither of these courses needs to be large in volume, because there are still three more to follow – meat or seafood, vegetables and dessert. But if this meal structure sounds daunting, it need not be. Many Italians eat only a 'full meal' on special occasions, or at the weekend, when there is more time to cook – and more time to talk, argue, laugh, savour and enjoy.

Enjoyment is the most characteristic aspect of Italian cooking and eating, and I hope that the recipes here will persuade you into the kitchen, that they will enhance your life, and give you endless pleasure.

the Italian storecupboard

The essence of Italian cooking, apart from its simplicity, is its freshness, and meat or fish, vegetables and fruit are bought daily in Italy and chosen according to the season. But there are certain essentials, which will be kept in the storecupboard or 'la dispensa' and renewed regularly when needed. The Italian storecupboard – indeed anyone's storecupboard – should be stocked so that the basics for a delicious meal are always at hand.

Pasta

Perhaps surprisingly, Italians tend to eat more dried pasta than fresh. Pasta is made at home, but usually only for special occasions. For the daily pasta course, the choice would normally be dried. I suggest you keep a selection of different types in your storecupboard: long pasta, such as tagliatelle and spaghetti; short pasta such as macaroni, conchiglie, farfalle and fusilli; and pastina or very small pasta shapes.

Choose the variety of pasta according to the sauce you intend to serve. Long ribbon pastas of varying thicknesses, such as tagliatelle, are best served with butter, tomato, cream and fish sauces. Spaghetti and linguine are matched by pesto, tomato, fish and meat sauces, including Bolognese of course. Short pasta shapes such as orecchiette and conchiglie, are best with vegetable sauces, the curves and indentations of the pasta ideal for holding small morsels of sauce. And the tiny shapes of pastina – from stellini to farfalline – are destined for soups.

Rice and grains

Italy relies on many grains, but the most important is wheat, which is made into flours for bread and pasta. Wheat flours come in a number of forms, graded by their fineness and suitability for different types of cooking. The best Italian storecupboard would contain farina '00' or doppio zero for making fresh pasta, pastry and cakes; '0' grade for pizza; and semolino duro, a ground durum wheat flour used in the making of commercial pasta and gnocchi. There would also be strong unbleached flour for bread-making, plain flour for pastry and self-raising flour for cakes. Farro is an ancient type of wheat also known as spelt. It is now enjoying a resurgence in popularity, and is being cultivated for use mainly in soups.

Rice, grown in the valley of the Po river and its tributaries in the north of Italy, is another staple. Risotto is the most famous of Italy's rice dishes and there are three main varieties of risotto rice available in this country – arborio, carnaroli and vialone nano. The principal characteristic of risotto rice is its ability to absorb moisture, thus enlarging the grain. The grain softens and develops a creamy texture, while retaining a bite, described as al dente (to the tooth). Rice is also used in soups, snacks, salads, stuffings and as a main course accompaniment.

The third most important grain for the storecupboard is polenta. This is made with a yellow maize or white corn flour. A staple in northern Italy, polenta is available in two forms. The one I prefer is the standard coarse grain, which needs up to 40 minutes to cook. The other is a quick-cook polenta that may not be quite as tasty, but is perfectly acceptable when enriched with butter and cheese. Polenta can be served 'wet', straight from the pan, as an accompaniment to a meat, mushroom or vegetable stew or sauce. Or it can be left until cold and set, then sliced and served instead of bread, or the slices may be fried or grilled to accompany meats, poultry or game birds, or sausages. Sometimes set polenta is enriched with butter, cheese and other flavourings.

Pulses

When in season, legumes or pulses are eaten fresh in Italy, but in this country they are most commonly found dried. With a packet of dried cannellini or borlotti beans, chick peas or Castelluccio lentils in your storecupboard, you will never be short of something to cook that will be nutritious and satisfying. Most pulses require long soaking to rehydrate them, and then take quite a time to cook. If you are short of time, however, canned pulses are a good alternative and make good standby items.

Nuts and seeds

These need to be bought fresh and used fairly regularly. Nuts and seeds, for instance, contain oils, which can turn rancid. Walnuts, hazelnuts, almonds and pine nuts are used extensively in Italian cooking, in both sweet and savoury dishes. Seeds, such as fennel, aniseed and sesame, make wonderful flavourings and garnishes, and they are highly nutritious.

Dried fruit

Keep a selection of organic ready-to-eat dried apricots, prunes, figs, raisins and sultanas in your storecupboard to use for breads, desserts and sweets.

Oils and butter

Olive oil is the bottled essence of Italy. It is used extensively here now, particularly since the virtues of the so-called 'Mediterranean diet' and its almost exclusive use of olive oil became known. Oils are graded according to acidity – extra virgin olive oil has the lowest acidity, is the purest and most flavourful. Thrifty housekeepers – whether from Umbria, Puglia, Tuscany or Liguria – will always have a bottle or two of the local new season's oil (available from November usually), which they will use only for dressings and as a condiment – sprinkled generously over a thick soup, for instance.

Extra virgin olive oil is best reserved for dressings. It is not used in cooking, as heat damages the proteins. Virgin olive oil is usually produced from more mature olives, is higher in acidity, and can be used for light cooking or in dressings such as mayonnaise. Straightforward olive oil is what you should use for cooking. This is also the oil to utilise for preserving vegetables or making a flavoured oil. I like to do this at Christmas time: olive oil in a nice bottle, with floating herbs, chillies and garlic, makes a good present for friends and family.

Unsalted butter is another Italian cooking medium, used mainly in the north, although it features in cake and biscuit making throughout the rest of the country.

Cheeses

The most vital cheese in the Italian storecupboard is Parmesan, as it has so many uses. It is perishable and should therefore be kept in the fridge, but it has a good shelf life. Keep a piece ready for grating, well wrapped in the salad drawer of the fridge to prevent it drying out. To use at its best, buy little and often.

Vinegars

A selection of vinegars will feature in any Italian storecupboard. Red and white wine vinegars are both used in cooking and salad dressings, but the most highly prized vinegar in Italy is balsamic or 'aceto balsamico'. This is probably the most expensive condiment in the Italian kitchen, because the maturation process is so lengthy and involved, but a drop or two of an aged balsamic can transform a dish. The finest balsamic vinegars, labelled 'aceto balsamico tradizionale di Modena', are over 30 years old, but you can buy less expensive and still exceptionally good balsamic vinegar aged from 5 to 20 years (similarly labelled but missing the word 'tradizionale').

Basic flavourings

The primary flavouring spices of any kitchen, including the Italian one, are salt, pepper and sugar. I always use sea salt (coarse and flake varieties, and fine table salt), and grind my pepper freshly from black peppercorns. Of the sugars, I keep golden caster, granulated, soft brown and icing sugar. I also store a vanilla pod in a container of caster sugar, so I always have some fragrant vanilla sugar to hand.

Herbs, spices and aromatics

Most Italian housekeepers would have fresh herbs almost constantly to hand in pots on the windowsill or in the garden – basil, flat leaf parsley, thyme, marjoram, sage and mint in particular. However, dried oregano is an essential storecupboard item, and one of the few herbs which is actually improved by drying. If you have oregano in the garden, you can dry small bunches in an airing cupboard, if you like. Dried bay leaves are also worth stocking, and you can dry these if you have a bay tree in the garden. Garlic is, of course, a vital flavouring in many Italian dishes, so you will need to keep a supply of fresh garlic bulbs.

Dried chillies are very popular in southern Italy and small, fiery red chillies, called peperoncini, appear in a variety of dishes. These are available dried, but should be used cautiously as they are very hot.

The other spices most commonly encountered are nutmeg, juniper berries, ground paprika, cinnamon, cloves and saffron. Keep whole nutmeg and grate freshly as required. Ready-ground spices should be bought and used frequently, as they lose flavour during lengthy storage. Saffron is best bought as threads as these are less liable to be adulterated than the powdered alternative. This revered and expensive spice is used for a classic risotto milanese. Vanilla pods and vanilla extract lend an inimitable flavour to many Italian desserts and ice creams.

Dried mushrooms

These are a primary source of flavour in the Italian kitchen and a packet or two of dried porcini or ceps is essential in the storecupboard. Fresh wild mushrooms are collected and eaten enthusiastically all over Italy in the autumn, but at other times of year, they are used dried – and lend extraordinary flavour to many dishes. Rehydrate by soaking in warm water to cover for about 20 minutes (strain and save the water for stock, as it will be full of flavour).

Other storecupboard essentials

There are so many important storecupboard items in an Italian kitchen, it is hard to name them all. The tomato, which is essential in lots of Italian dishes, will be on the shelves in various guises. Canned plum tomatoes, whole or chopped (often with added herbs), sit alongside passata (cooked puréed tomatoes), sun-dried tomatoes and, perhaps, sun-dried tomato paste.

Artichokes are preserved in oil, capers are brined or salted, and anchovies are salted or preserved in oil. (The salt from capers and anchovies must be rinsed off before use.) Olives are preserved in brine or oil, often with other flavourings; my favourite is the Gaeta olive. Truffles flavour oils or are condensed with ceps to make an expensive, but delicious, paste. A can or two of tuna, in brine or oil, can be used in a matter of moments to make a salad or sauce.

On the sweet side, I like to have jars of apricot jam and honey available – good on breakfast toast, or in baking and desserts. I'm not a chocoholic, but some good dark chocolate is great in puddings, as is cocoa powder. Even the coffee beans so vital for the espresso, can be used in cooking. And I always keep amaretti biscuits, to serve with coffee, use in my dessert recipes, or crumble over ice cream.

The Italian storecupboard should also boast a limited selection of alcohol. Red and white wines, vermouth, Marsala and Vin Santo, and spirits such as brandy and the uniquely Italian grappa, add flavour and character to many sauces and desserts.

easy
antipasti

Stuffed mussels

Serves 4

1kg (2¼lb) fresh mussels
2 unwaxed lemons, cut into quarters
4 garlic cloves, peeled
3 tbsp dry white wine
4 tbsp olive oil

large handful of flat leaf parsley,
  finely chopped
125g (4oz) fresh white breadcrumbs
  (slightly dry)
sea salt and pepper
lemon wedges, to serve

1 Preheat the oven to 220°C (fan oven 200°C), gas mark 7. Discard any broken mussels, and those that do not close when sharply tapped. Scrub the mussels thoroughly in cold water and pull out the little beards.

2 Put the lemon quarters, garlic and white wine into a large sauté pan or wide saucepan. Add the mussels, cover with a tight-fitting lid and cook over a high heat for 5 minutes until the shells open, shaking the pan from time to time. Discard any mussels that remain closed.

3 Using a slotted spoon, remove the mussels from the pan, reserving the liquor. Remove and discard the empty half shells. Loosen the mussels in the bottom shells and place the shells on a baking sheet.

4 Filter the reserved cooking liquor through a muslin-lined strainer into a bowl. Mix in the olive oil, parsley, breadcrumbs and salt and pepper to taste.

5 Spoon a little of the parsley and breadcrumb mixture over each mussel. Bake in the oven for about 7 minutes until the topping is golden brown. Serve hot, with lemon wedges.

A tasty classic from Campania, best served with a wedge of lemon for a simple antipasto. Other ingredients, such as chopped tomato and capers can be added to the stuffing.

Warm seafood salad

Illustrated on previous pages

Serves 6

500g (1lb 2oz) fresh mussels

2 tbsp dry white wine

1 dried chilli

500g (1lb 2oz) squid, cleaned

2 tbsp white wine vinegar

1 onion, peeled and halved

2 bay leaves

500g (1lb 2oz) monkfish fillet, skinned

6 scallops, shelled and cleaned

12 large raw prawns in shell

sea salt and pepper

handful of black olives, to serve

For the dressing

1 garlic clove, peeled and crushed

handful of flat leaf parsley, finely chopped

3 tbsp lemon juice

3 tbsp virgin olive oil

1 Discard any broken mussels, and those that do not close when sharply tapped. Scrub the mussels thoroughly in cold water and pull out the beards, then place in a large saucepan with the wine. Cover and cook over a high heat for about 4 minutes until they open, shaking the pan occasionally. Lift out the mussels with a slotted spoon, discarding any that remain closed. When cool enough to handle, shell the mussels and place in a bowl. Pour the cooking liquor through a muslin-lined strainer on to the mussels. Add the dried chilli, stir and set aside.

2 Rinse the squid well and cut the pouches into 1cm (½ inch) rings, keeping the tentacles whole (if available). Put 1.5 litres (2½ pints) water into a saucepan with 1 tbsp of the vinegar, the onion, 1 bay leaf and some salt, and bring to the boil. Add the squid and cook at a steady simmer until opaque and you can pierce them with a fork, about 5 minutes depending on size. Remove with a slotted spoon, drain well and add to the mussels.

3 Cut the monkfish into large chunks and add to the water in which the squid was cooked. Simmer gently for about 2 minutes. Remove from the heat, leaving the fish in the liquid.

4 Meanwhile, heat 300ml (½ pint) water in another pan with the remaining bay leaf and vinegar, and some salt. When it comes to the boil, add the scallops and simmer gently for 2 minutes. Remove with a slotted spoon and set aside with the mussels and squid. Add the prawns to the scallop cooking water, bring to a simmer and cook for 1 minute. Drain and, when cool enough to handle, peel, leaving the tail shell on if you like. Drain the monkfish and add to the other seafood with the prawns. Remove and discard the chilli.

5 For the dressing, combine the garlic, parsley and lemon juice in a small bowl. Add a generous grinding of black pepper and some salt. Whisk in the olive oil, then taste and adjust the seasoning. Toss the seafood with the dressing and divide between shallow bowls. Serve immediately, while still warm, scattered with the olives.

Every region of Italy has its own version of this seafood salad, which is best served warm. You can vary the fish, but do include a variety of textures, avoiding oily fish, as the flavour would be too pronounced.

Marinated and grilled sardines

Serves 4

8 fresh sardines, cleaned and heads removed

6 tbsp olive oil

2 tbsp white wine vinegar

2 garlic cloves, peeled and crushed

1 red chilli, deseeded and chopped

2 tbsp finely chopped parsley

lemon wedges, to serve

1 Place the sardines in a shallow dish. Mix the olive oil, wine vinegar, garlic, chilli and parsley together and pour over the sardines. Leave to marinate for 1 hour, turning once.

2 Preheat the grill (or barbecue). Remove the sardines from the marinade and place on the grill rack. Drizzle with the marinade. Cook for 12 minutes, turning once and basting occasionally with the marinade.

3 Serve hot, drizzled with the pan juices and accompanied by lemon wedges.

Seafood antipasti are popular in coastal areas of Italy, not least those featuring sardines. Vary the flavourings in this marinade to taste, perhaps adding thinly sliced red onion, or capers and grated lemon zest.

Chicken liver crostini

Serves 6–8

250g (9oz) chicken livers
2 tbsp olive oil
1 celery stalk, finely chopped
1 shallot, peeled and very finely
  chopped
2 small garlic cloves, peeled and
  chopped
generous handful of flat leaf parsley,
  chopped

125g (4oz) lean beef mince
1 tbsp tomato purée
6 tbsp dry white wine
12–16 slices of ciabatta bread
1 tbsp capers, rinsed and chopped
2 salted anchovy fillets, rinsed and
  finely chopped
100g (3½oz) unsalted butter
extra virgin olive oil, to drizzle
sea salt and pepper

1 Trim the fat and gristle from the chicken livers, then rinse, pat dry with kitchen paper and chop finely. Set aside.

2 Heat the olive oil in a saucepan and, when just hot, add the celery, shallot, garlic and parsley. Cook for about 10 minutes until soft, stirring frequently.

3 Add the chicken livers and beef mince and cook over a very low heat until the livers have lost their raw colour and become crumbly. Mix in the tomato purée and cook for 1 minute.

4 Increase the heat, pour in the wine and boil to reduce until almost totally evaporated. Lower the heat and add a little salt and plenty of pepper. Simmer for 30 minutes, adding a little hot water if the mixture becomes too dry.

5 Meanwhile, preheat the oven to 180°C (fan oven 160°C), gas mark 4. To make the crostini, bake the ciabatta slices until crisp and golden, about 10–12 minutes.

6 Add the capers and anchovies to the chicken liver mixture. Mix in the butter and cook gently for 5 minutes, stirring constantly. Moisten the crostini with a little extra virgin olive oil, then spread with the chicken liver mixture. Serve at once.

Ciabatta crostini are the norm in Tuscany for this robust antipasta dish, but you can use bruschetta (page 32) if you prefer, allowing one per person.

Bruschetta

Makes 6

6 slices of coarse white Italian bread, preferably Pugliese, about 3cm (1¼ inches) thick

2 garlic cloves, peeled and halved

about 6 tbsp extra virgin olive oil, to drizzle

sea salt and pepper

1 Preheat the grill or a griddle pan and heat the oven to 220°C (fan oven 200°C), gas mark 7. Score the bread slices lightly with the point of a small knife in a criss-cross fashion, then grill or griddle to toast on both sides.
2 While still hot, rub the toasted surface all over with the cut garlic cloves. Put the toast slices on a baking sheet and bake in the oven for 2 minutes to crisp them through.
3 Drizzle about 1 tbsp extra virgin oil over each slice. Sprinkle generously with pepper and a little salt, then serve.

Bruschetta are slices of rustic bread, baked until crisp and slightly charred, then rubbed with garlic and drizzled with olive oil. Usually served as an appetiser, they are also very good with fish soups and pan-fried chicken livers.

Broad bean purée

Illustrated on previous pages

Serves 6–8

500g (1lb 2oz) podded fresh or
    frozen broad beans
2 garlic cloves, peeled
50g (2oz) crustless white bread
about 2 tbsp milk
5 tbsp extra virgin olive oil
sea salt and pepper

For the crostini

12–16 slices of ciabatta bread
extra virgin olive oil, to drizzle

1 Cook the fresh or frozen beans in a saucepan of simmering water, to which you have added 1 garlic clove, at a low simmer for about 5 minutes. When the beans are tender, drain them and the garlic, reserving 2 tbsp of the liquid. Set aside to cool.

2 Place the bread in a bowl and pour on enough milk to moisten it. Slip the broad beans out of their white skins and discard the skins. This will give you a really creamy purée.

3 Put the bright emerald beans, both garlic cloves and the bread with its milk into a food processor. Whiz to a purée, gradually adding the olive oil through the funnel. If the purée is very thick, add a little of the reserved bean cooking liquid. Taste and adjust the seasoning.

4 For the crostini, preheat the oven to 180°C (fan oven 160°C), gas mark 4. Bake the ciabatta slices until crisp and golden, about 10–12 minutes. Moisten the crostini with a little extra virgin olive oil, then serve with the broad bean purée.

Enjoy this wonderful purée during the very brief early summer broad bean season. It is delicious spread on crostini moistened with olive oil, or on bruschetta (page 32), or you can serve it as a dip with crudités.

Roasted pepper and tuna salad

Serves 4–6

2 red peppers
2 yellow peppers
6 plum tomatoes
½ ciabatta loaf
8 tbsp extra virgin olive oil
400g can tuna in spring water,
   drained and flaked

2 tbsp chopped parsley
2 tbsp chopped basil
2 tbsp chopped capers
12 black olives, pitted
2 tbsp red wine vinegar
sea salt and pepper

1 Preheat the oven to 200°C (fan oven 180°C), gas mark 6. Put the red and yellow peppers on a baking tray and roast for 20 minutes. Leave until cool enough to handle, then peel away the skins. Halve, core and deseed the peppers, then cut into strips, saving the juices.

2 Immerse the tomatoes in boiling water for 10 seconds, then drain and peel away the skins. Quarter, core and deseed the tomatoes, then chop the flesh.

3 Tear the bread into cubes, put into a bowl and moisten with half of the olive oil and the roasted pepper juices. Add the peppers, tomatoes and flaked tuna and mix gently. Scatter over the herbs, capers and olives.

4 Drizzle the wine vinegar and the rest of the extra virgin olive oil over the salad, season well with salt and pepper, and toss gently to serve.

I love the variety of textures, colours and flavours in this simple antipasto – designed to bring the tastebuds to anticipatory life.

Char-grilled aubergine on rocket salad

Serves 4

100g (3½oz) wild rocket leaves

12 tbsp ready-prepared preserved char-grilled aubergine slices, drained

8 sun-dried tomatoes in oil, drained and chopped

8 anchovy fillets, rinsed if salted

12 black or green olives, pitted

Parmesan cheese shavings, to serve

1 Arrange the rocket leaves on serving plates and lay the char-grilled aubergine slices on top. Sprinkle the chopped sun-dried tomatoes, anchovies and olives over the leaves and aubergine.

2 Scatter some Parmesan cheese shavings over the salad and serve, with grissini (breadsticks) if you like.

Now that you can buy ready-prepared Italian foods such as char-grilled aubergine slices, preserved artichoke hearts and salted anchovies from supermarkets, you can create tasty antipasti with the minimum of effort.

Prosciutto with fresh figs and mozzarella

Serves 4
8 slices of prosciutto
2 ripe, fresh figs, halved vertically
150g (5oz) fresh buffalo mozzarella
   cheese

2–3 tsp aged balsamic vinegar
2 tbsp extra virgin olive oil
large handful of pine nuts, toasted
sea salt and pepper

1 Drape 2 slices of prosciutto on each serving plate and top with a fresh fig half. Tear the fresh buffalo mozzarella into pieces and place alongside.
2 Dress the mozzarella with a little aged balsamic vinegar and extra virgin olive oil, then sprinkle with the toasted pine nuts.
3 Season the mozzarella with a little salt and a generous grinding of black pepper, then serve the antipasto, with grissini (breadsticks).

I love this combination of colours, flavours and textures. Ripe, flavourful fresh figs are essential and real buffalo mozzarella will make all the difference to this antipasto.

Artichoke, chick pea and baby spinach salad

Serves 4–6

400g can chick peas, drained and rinsed

280g jar of artichokes in oil, drained and quartered

1 red onion, peeled and finely chopped

2 good handfuls of baby spinach leaves

12 black olives, halved and pitted

For the dressing

juice of 1 lemon

6 tbsp extra virgin olive oil

sea salt and pepper

1 Combine the chick peas, quartered artichokes and red onion in a bowl. Add the baby spinach and black olives, and mix lightly.

2 For the dressing, whisk the lemon juice and olive oil and season with a little salt and pepper.

3 Drizzle the dressing over the salad and toss gently to mix. Arrange on individual plates and serve.

This simple antipasto can be assembled in minutes. Tear a little buffalo mozzarella over the salad to serve if you like.

Tomatoes stuffed with herb breadcrumbs

Illustrated on previous pages

Serves 4

6 large, ripe but firm, tomatoes
  (preferably with stalks)
olive oil, to brush
handful of flat leaf parsley, chopped
2 garlic cloves, peeled and chopped
1 tbsp capers, rinsed and chopped
½ small dried hot chilli, crumbled

100g (3½oz) fresh white
  breadcrumbs (slightly dry)
1 tsp dried oregano
1 tbsp extra virgin olive oil, plus
  extra to drizzle
sea salt and pepper
freshly grated Parmesan cheese, to
  serve (optional)

1 Cut the tops off the tomatoes and reserve. Scoop out the core and seeds, then sprinkle the cavities with salt. Lay the tomatoes, cut-side down, on kitchen paper and leave to drain for about 30 minutes.

2 Preheat the oven to 190°C (fan oven 170°C), gas mark 5. Brush the base of a shallow baking dish or roasting tin with a little olive oil. Wipe the inside of the tomatoes with kitchen paper.

3 Combine the parsley, garlic, capers, chilli, breadcrumbs and oregano in a bowl. Mix well, then stir in the extra virgin olive oil. Season with salt and pepper to taste.

4 Stand the tomatoes, cut-side up, in the prepared dish and spoon in the stuffing. Replace the tomato lids and bake in the oven for about 20 minutes until the tomatoes are soft but still whole.

5 If liked, lift the tomato lids, drizzle a little olive oil over the stuffing and sprinkle lightly with grated Parmesan. Serve hot, warm or at room temperature.

Flavourful, ripe tomatoes are essential for this classic Roman antipasto dish. Make it in advance if you like, to allow time for the flavours to combine and intensify. Serve hot, warm or cold, but not chilled.

Sicilian baked stuffed aubergines

Serves 4

2 medium aubergines

4 tbsp olive oil, plus extra to drizzle

1 large garlic clove, peeled and
crushed

2 shallots, peeled and finely chopped

1 celery stalk, chopped

250g (9oz) spicy pork sausage,
skinned

125g (4oz) fresh white breadcrumbs

2 tbsp pine nuts

2 tbsp capers, rinsed and dried

1 egg, beaten

2 tsp dried oregano

2 tbsp freshly grated Parmesan
cheese

1 tbsp currants

1 large ripe tomato, cut into strips

sea salt and pepper

1 Cut the aubergines in half lengthways. Scoop out the flesh, using a small
sharp knife and then a small teaspoon, leaving a thin layer inside the skin.
Be careful not to pierce the skin.

2 Chop the aubergine pulp coarsely and place in a colander. Sprinkle with
salt, mix well and set aside to drain for 20 minutes.

3 Heat 3 tbsp of the olive oil in a frying pan. Add the garlic, shallots and
celery, and sauté over a low heat until soft, stirring frequently. Add the
sausagemeat, in small pieces, and cook for 20 minutes, turning frequently.

4 Meanwhile, preheat the oven to 180°C (fan oven 160°C), gas mark 4.
Squeeze the liquid from the aubergine pulp, rinse to remove excess salt,
drain and pat dry with kitchen paper. Add the aubergine pulp to the pan and
fry gently, stirring, for a few minutes. Taste and adjust the seasoning.

5 Add the breadcrumbs to the pan and cook, stirring, for 2–3 minutes. Stir
in the pine nuts and cook for a further 30 seconds, then transfer to a bowl.
Add the capers, egg, oregano, Parmesan, currants and salt and pepper. Mix
thoroughly, taste and adjust the seasoning.

6 Oil a deep baking dish with the remaining 1 tbsp olive oil. Pat the inside of
the aubergine shells dry, then place side by side in the dish and fill with the
sausage mixture. Lay the tomato strips on the top and drizzle with a little
olive oil. Pour 150ml (¼ pint) water into the bottom of the dish. Cover with
foil and bake for 20 minutes, then remove the foil and bake for a further
20 minutes. Serve the dish warm, an hour after you take it from the oven.

Braised shallots

Serves 4
750g (1lb 10oz) shallots
3 tbsp olive oil
25g (1oz) unsalted butter
2 tsp tomato purée

1 tbsp caster sugar
2 tbsp red wine vinegar
250g (9oz) seedless black grapes
sea salt and pepper

1 Add the shallots to a saucepan of boiling water, bring back to the boil and blanch for 1 minute. Drain well and remove the skins and root ends, taking care to keep the root base intact, as this will hold the shallot together during cooking.
2 Heat the olive oil and butter in a large sauté pan. Add the shallots and sauté for about 12 minutes until golden, shaking the pan frequently.
3 Dissolve the tomato purée in 2 tsp of hot water and add to the pan with the sugar, vinegar, grapes and salt and pepper. Cook, uncovered, for about 25 minutes until the shallots are tender and a nice brown colour, adding a little water if necessary. Serve the shallots hot or cold, but not chilled.

Braised onions or shallots are often served hot or cold as part of a Piedmontese antipasto. They may also accompany cold meats, or you can serve them hot with braised meat dishes.

Stuffed mushrooms

Serves 4

50g (2oz) dried porcini mushrooms
4 large field mushrooms (or large chestnut mushrooms)
2 anchovy fillets in oil, drained
1 garlic clove, peeled
handful of marjoram leaves
100g (3½oz) fresh white breadcrumbs
pinch of freshly grated nutmeg
2 tbsp olive oil, plus extra to drizzle
handful of flat leaf parsley, finely chopped
sea salt and pepper

1 Soak the dried porcini in warm water to cover for 10 minutes. Drain and pat dry with kitchen paper. (Save the soaking water to use as stock for another dish if you like.)

2 Preheat the oven to 200°C (fan oven 180°C), gas mark 6. Gently wipe the fresh mushrooms with damp kitchen paper to clean them. Detach the stems and reserve.

3 Chop the soaked porcini, mushroom stems, anchovies, garlic and marjoram together. Tip into a bowl and add the breadcrumbs, nutmeg and salt and pepper to taste. Mix thoroughly.

4 Heat the olive oil in a frying pan over a medium heat. Add the mushroom and breadcrumb mixture and sauté for 5 minutes.

5 Lay the mushroom caps on an oiled baking sheet, hollow-side up. Season lightly with salt and then fill them with the crumb mixture. Sprinkle parsley on top of each stuffed mushroom and drizzle with a little olive oil. Bake for about 10–15 minutes until soft. Serve at room temperature.

A wonderful combination of intense flavours – anchovy, nutmeg, garlic and marjoram – is piled into big mushrooms and baked to serve as an antipasto.

Duck breasts with balsamic vinegar

Serves 6

2 duck breasts, each about
   400g (14oz)
3 heads of radicchio

3 tbsp aged balsamic vinegar, or a
   little more to taste
sea salt and pepper

1 Cut the duck breasts in half widthways. Score the skin with the tip of a small sharp knife, then rub with salt and pepper.

2 Heat a heavy-based frying pan. Place the duck breasts in the pan, skin-side down, and cook over a medium heat for about 9 minutes, depending on thickness. Pour most of the rendered fat from the pan. (Save it for sautéeing potatoes if you like.)

3 Meanwhile, preheat the grill. Quarter the radicchio and place on a lightly oiled baking tray. Grill for 7–10 minutes, turning occasionally, until slightly charred all over.

4 Spoon 1 tbsp balsamic vinegar over the duck breasts, then turn and cook for 2 minutes on the other side. Lift out the duck breasts on to a board, cover with foil and set aside in a warm place to rest for 10 minutes.

5 In the meantime, add the remaining balsamic vinegar and 3 tbsp warm water to the frying pan and stir well to deglaze, scraping up the sediment from the bottom of the pan. Taste for seasoning and add a little more balsamic vinegar if required.

6 Carve the duck crossways into 1cm (½ inch) slices and arrange on warm plates, with the char-grilled radicchio alongside. Drizzle the balsamic pan juices over the duck breast slices and serve.

Duck is very popular in Italy and it is tastes particularly good dressed with balsamic vinegar and served on a bed of char-grilled radicchio, or crisp rocket leaves if you prefer.

Mozzarella fritters with roasted tomatoes

Serves 4

250g (9oz) mozzarella cheese, drained 24 hours in advance and chilled (to dry slightly)

125g (4oz) Parmesan cheese, freshly grated

2 tbsp Italian '00' flour

1 large egg, lightly beaten

generous handful of basil leaves, torn

1 garlic clove, peeled and crushed

4 tbsp olive oil

sea salt and pepper

For the roasted cherry tomatoes

250g (9oz) cherry tomatoes, on the vine

olive oil, to drizzle

1 Preheat the oven to 180°C (fan oven 160°C), gas mark 4. Shred the mozzarella, using a coarse cheese grater, and place in a bowl. Add the Parmesan and flour and toss to mix, then add the beaten egg to bind, mixing thoroughly.

2 Add the torn basil, garlic and some salt and pepper, and mix well. With damp hands, shape the mixture into balls, the size of a walnut. Place on a tray and chill in the fridge for 30 minutes.

3 Place the cherry tomatoes (still on the vine) on an oiled baking tray, drizzle with a little olive oil and roast in the oven for 20 minutes until the skins split.

4 Meanwhile, heat the 4 tbsp olive oil in a large frying pan. Fry the mozzarella fritters in batches, for about 10 minutes, turning until golden all over. Remove with a slotted spoon and drain on kitchen paper. Keep warm while you cook the rest.

5 Drizzle the roasted cherry tomatoes with a little more olive oil and season well with salt and pepper. Serve the fritters hot, with the roasted tomatoes.

These intensely flavoured cheesy bites are served with roasted cherry tomatoes on the vine. They are very popular with children.

Piemontese fondue

Serves 4
400g (14oz) Italian fontina cheese
275ml (9fl oz) whole milk
125g (4oz) unsalted butter
4 egg yolks

1 tbsp truffle paste (optional)
freshly ground black pepper
For the crostini
12–16 slices of ciabatta bread

1 About 4 hours ahead of serving, cut the fontina into small dice. Place in a bowl, add enough of the milk to cover the cheese and set aside.

2 Preheat the oven to 180°C (fan oven 160°C), gas mark 4. Put the butter into a large heatproof bowl over a pan of simmering water, and add the fontina and all of the milk. Cook, stirring constantly, until the cheese has melted, about 10 minutes.

3 Meanwhile, for the crostini, bake the ciabatta slices until crisp and golden, about 10–12 minutes.

4 Beat the egg yolks into the smooth cheese mixture, one at a time. Continue to cook over the pan of simmering water, beating constantly, until the fondue is the consistency of thick cream. Season with a generous grinding of black pepper and remove from the heat. If you happen to be adding truffle paste, stir it in at this point.

5 Transfer the fondue to warm individual bowls and serve the crostini to accompany.

Fontina cheese is the main ingredient of a classic fonduta piemontese. The other essential flavouring is white truffle. Fresh white truffle is prohibitively expensive, but you can buy truffle paste made with white truffles and porcini, which works very well in this recipe.

easy
soups and broths

Vegetable broth

Makes about 1.5 litres (2½ pints)

1 tbsp olive oil
40g (1½oz) unsalted butter
3 garlic cloves, peeled and crushed
1 large onion, peeled and coarsely
  chopped
4 leeks, trimmed, washed and
  coarsely chopped

2 carrots, peeled and coarsely
  chopped
2 celery stalks, coarsely chopped
1 fennel bulb, halved
handful of chopped flat leaf parsley
4 bay leaves
2 thyme sprigs
sea salt and pepper

1 Heat the olive oil and butter in a large saucepan or stock pot. Add the
garlic and fry gently for 2 minutes. Add the onion, leeks, carrots, celery,
fennel and herbs. Cook over a low heat, stirring constantly, until the
vegetables are softened, but not browned.

2 Add 3 litres (5 pints) water and bring to the boil. Reduce the heat, cover
and simmer for 1 hour. Strain the broth and return to the pan, discarding
the vegetables and herbs. Boil rapidly until reduced by half, then season
with salt and pepper to taste. Allow to cool.

3 Keep the broth refrigerated and use within 3 days, or freeze.

A good, fine flavoured broth – vegetable, fish
or chicken stock – is the basis for most Italian
soups, savoury sauces and risottos. The
aromatic vegetables and herbs can be varied,
but they should always be in good condition.

Chicken broth

Makes about 1.5 litres (2½ pints)
1 free-range chicken, about
   1.4kg (3lb)
2 onions, peeled
2 celery stalks
1 large potato, peeled and quartered

4 bay leaves
handful of flat leaf parsley (leaves
   and stalks)
2 thyme sprigs
sea salt and pepper

1 Rinse the chicken in cold water, drain well and cut off any visible fat.
Bring 3.4 litres (6 pints) water to the boil in a very large saucepan or stock
pot over a high heat. Add the chicken to the pan along with the onions,
celery, potato and herbs. Bring to the boil and boil rapidly for 5 minutes.
2 Reduce the heat to low and simmer very slowly, uncovered, for about
2 hours. Skim off any scum from the surface from time to time. Remove the
chicken, then strain the broth through a fine sieve into a bowl and season
with salt and pepper to taste. Allow to cool, then chill the broth.
3 Once chilled, remove the solidified fat that has accumulated on the surface.
Keep the broth refrigerated and use within 5 days, or freeze.

A chicken broth should ideally be made with a
good raw chicken, although a slightly less
flavoursome broth can be made with a raw
carcass (or a cooked carcass left from a roast).

Fish broth

Makes about 1.2 litres (2 pints)

1kg (2¼lb) white fish heads and
   bones
10 cloves
2 onions, peeled
2 carrots
2 celery stalks
2 bay leaves
10 black peppercorns
1½ tsp salt
500ml (16 fl oz) dry white wine

1 Put the fish heads and bones into a large saucepan. Press the cloves into the onions and add to the pan with the carrots, celery, bay leaves, black peppercorns, salt and white wine. Add 2 litres (3½ pints) water and bring to the boil.

2 Simmer, uncovered, for 30 minutes until the broth is well reduced. Strain the liquid through a fine sieve, discarding the bones and aromatics. Allow to cool, then chill.

3 Keep the broth refrigerated and use within 2 days, or freeze.

A fish broth must be made with white fish bones; those from oily fish are not suitable. When you buy fresh fish, ask for the bones and perhaps an extra white fish head or two to make your broth.

Minestrone

Serves 6

1.5 litres (2½ pints) chicken broth (page 64)
2 tbsp olive oil
1 onion, peeled and finely chopped
3 bay leaves
2 garlic cloves, peeled and chopped
handful of flat leaf parsley, chopped
2 celery stalks, trimmed and sliced
2 large carrots, peeled and roughly chopped
1 parsnip, peeled and roughly chopped
2 leeks, washed, trimmed and finely sliced
200g (7oz) podded fresh or frozen peas (preferably fresh)
12 strands of dried spaghetti, broken into short lengths
2 tbsp sweet vermouth
sea salt and pepper

1 Pour the chicken broth into a large saucepan and bring to a simmer.

2 Heat the olive oil in another large saucepan, add the onion and sauté gently for about 5 minutes until golden. Add the bay leaves, garlic and parsley and stir. Add the celery, carrots, parsnip and leeks, and sauté until slightly softened.

3 Add the warmed chicken broth to the pan and bring to the boil. Add the peas, pasta and vermouth, and simmer for 20 minutes until the vegetables are all tender. Taste for seasoning, then serve, in warm bowls with country-style bread.

In Italy, the ingredients for this soup will be determined by the contents of the larder. A little spaghetti and plenty of fresh parsley are vital, but you can use whatever vegetables happen to be in the kitchen.

Lettuce in broth

Serves 6

25g (1oz) dried porcini mushrooms

125g (4oz) coarse, fresh white
  breadcrumbs (slightly dry)

3 tbsp milk

6 Little Gem lettuces

2 garlic cloves, peeled and chopped

2 tbsp chopped marjoram leaves

25g (1oz) Parmesan cheese, freshly
  grated

2 eggs, beaten

1 egg white, beaten

6 or 12 slices of firm, coarse-
  textured bread

6 tbsp extra virgin olive oil

1.5 litres (2½ pints) chicken broth
  (page 64) or vegetable broth
  (page 61)

sea salt and pepper

1 Preheat the oven to 180°C (fan oven 160°C), gas mark 4. Soak the dried
porcini in warm water for 10 minutes, then drain and chop. Soak the
breadcrumbs in the milk for 5 minutes, then squeeze dry. Discard the
outermost leaves from the lettuces, then carefully extract the hearts, keeping
the heads intact.

2 Chop two of the lettuce hearts and place in a bowl (save the rest for a
salad). Add the porcini, garlic, breadcrumbs and marjoram. Mix in the
Parmesan, beaten whole eggs and seasoning.

3 Blanch the lettuce heads in a pan of boiling water for a few seconds. Drain,
open carefully and fill with the prepared stuffing. Re-close, brushing with
the beaten egg white to seal and hold in the filling.

4 Brush the bread slices liberally with 5 tbsp olive oil, place on a baking
sheet and toast in the oven for about 10 minutes. Meanwhile, heat the
remaining olive oil and 4 tbsp of the broth in a wide saucepan, add the
stuffed lettuces and cook, covered, for a few minutes over a low heat,
turning occasionally. Bring the rest of the broth to the boil in another pan.
Put one or two toast slices into each warm soup bowl, add a stuffed lettuce
and pour the hot broth over to serve.

Stuffed vegetables are a source of pride in
Liguria. Here lettuce leaves are stuffed with
dried porcini, Parmesan, fresh marjoram and
breadcrumbs, then cooked in a fine broth.

Tuscan leek and tomato soup

Serves 6

8 young leeks, trimmed

50ml (2 fl oz) olive oil

675g (1½lb) ripe tomatoes

½ tsp dried red chilli flakes

250g (9 oz) crusty day-old bread

750ml (1¼ pints) chicken broth (page 64) or vegetable broth (page 61)

6 basil leaves

extra virgin olive oil, to drizzle

sea salt and pepper

1 Wash the leeks well under cold running water. Drain, then chop finely. Heat the olive oil in a large saucepan, add the chopped leeks and fry gently for 10 minutes.

2 Meanwhile, whiz the tomatoes in a blender or food processor to a purée (then sieve to remove skins and seeds if you prefer, though this isn't essential). Add to the leeks with the chilli and some salt and pepper. Bring to the boil and simmer for 20 minutes.

3 Break the bread into small pieces and add to the pan. Stir well and simmer gently for 5 minutes. Pour in the broth, mix well and simmer for a further 10 minutes.

4 Pour the soup into warm bowls and add a basil leaf to each serving. Drizzle with a little extra virgin olive oil and serve.

This is based on a classic Tuscan recipe. The inclusion of bread is typically Italian – even when stale, bread is never wasted and it adds texture to a soup.

La ribollita

Serves 6

175g (6oz) dried cannellini beans, soaked in cold water overnight

4 tbsp olive oil

1 large onion, peeled and finely sliced

4 carrots, peeled and chopped

4 celery stalks, chopped

4 leeks, washed, trimmed and chopped

2 garlic cloves, peeled and crushed

250g (9oz) cavolo nero, tough stalks discarded, leaves chopped

8 ripe tomatoes, skinned, deseeded and quartered

1 dried chilli, crumbled (with seeds)

1.5 litres (2½ pints) vegetable broth (page 61), or water

small handful of chopped flat leaf parsley

1 rosemary sprig, finely chopped

2 bay leaves

sea salt and pepper

To serve

8 slices of country-style bread

extra virgin olive oil (preferably new season's, estate bottled), to drizzle

3 tbsp chopped flat leaf parsley

1 Drain the cannellini beans and rinse under fresh cold water. Place in a large saucepan, cover generously with cold water and bring to the boil. Lower the heat, cover and simmer gently for about 1½ hours until the beans are just tender.

2 Heat half the olive oil in a large heavy-based pan, add the onion, cover and sweat for 5 minutes to soften. Add the carrots, celery, leeks and half of the garlic and sweat for a further 5 minutes. Add the cabbage, tomatoes and chilli and stir to coat in the oil. Add the beans and vegetable broth or water and simmer for 30 minutes or until the beans are soft.

3 Ladle a third of the soup mixture into a blender or food processor and whiz to a purée. Pour this back into the pan and stir to mix.

4 Heat the remaining 2 tbsp olive oil in a separate pan and sauté the other crushed garlic clove with the chopped herbs and bay leaves until lightly browned. Add to the soup, allow to cool and refrigerate for 24 hours.

5 The next day, warm the soup through in an uncovered pan and check the seasoning. Place a slice of bread in each warm soup bowl and ladle the ribollita over the top. Drizzle with a generous amount of extra virgin olive oil and sprinkle with sea salt and chopped parsley to serve.

Onion and chick pea soup

Serves 6

200g (7oz) dried chick peas, soaked overnight
300g (11oz) ripe tomatoes
4 tbsp olive oil
1kg (2¼lb) onions, peeled and sliced

1 celery stalk, chopped
50g (2oz) unsmoked bacon, diced
handful of basil leaves, torn
6 slices of firm, coarse-textured bread
sea salt and pepper

1 Drain and rinse the chick peas. Purée the tomatoes through a food mill or in a blender, then sieve.

2 Heat the olive oil in a large saucepan, add the onions, celery and bacon and fry gently for about 5 minutes until the onion is translucent. Add the puréed tomatoes, chick peas and 2 litres (3½ pints) water. Bring to the boil, lower the heat and simmer for 2 hours. Season and add add most of the basil.

3 When ready to serve, toast the bread slices on both sides and place a slice in each warm soup bowl. Pour the hot soup on top and sprinkle with the remaining torn basil.

This tasty soup of onions, chick peas, fresh tomatoes, bacon and bread keeps well and tastes even better a day or two after it is made.

Farro and bean soup

Serves 6

250g (9oz) dried borlotti beans,
  soaked in cold water overnight
200g (7oz) farro, soaked in cold
  water overnight
2 white onions, peeled
6 sage leaves
3 garlic cloves, peeled
4 tbsp olive oil

1 red onion, peeled and finely chopped
2 carrots, scraped and diced
2–4 celery stalks, trimmed and diced
handful of flat leaf parsley, chopped
275g (10oz) canned Italian plum
  tomatoes, with their juice
sea salt and pepper
extra virgin olive oil, to drizzle

1 Drain and rinse the borlotti beans, then place in a large saucepan with
1 whole white onion, 3 sage leaves, 1 garlic clove and enough water to cover
by at least 5cm (2 inches). Bring to the boil, lower the heat, cover and
simmer for 1 hour or until tender.

2 When the beans are cooked, pass half of the contents of the pan through a
food mill or purée in a blender or food processor and set aside. Keep the
whole beans in the pan.

3 Finely chop the other white onion and the remaining garlic. Heat the olive
oil in a large saucepan, add the chopped red and white onion, the carrots,
celery and garlic. Stir well, then add most of the parsley, the remaining
3 sage leaves, tomatoes and 3 tbsp water. Continue to cook, stirring
occasionally, for 10 minutes.

4 Drain and rinse the farro and add to the tomato mixture along with the
whole borlotti beans. Bring to a simmer and simmer over a low heat for
20 minutes. Add the puréed bean mixture and season with salt and pepper.
Heat, stirring, until thoroughly warmed through.

5 Taste and adjust the seasoning and ladle into warm bowls. Serve topped
with a generous drizzle of extra virgin olive oil and the remaining parsley.

Farro, a form of spelt or soft wheat, is an
ancient grain, grown in Tuscany. It readily
absorbs flavours and, combined with borlotti
beans, makes a wonderfully satisfying soup.

Fennel soup with roasted tomatoes

Illustrated on previous pages

Serves 4
4 fennel bulbs
1 tbsp olive oil
1.5 litres (2½ pints) vegetable broth
   (page 61)
1 tsp fennel seeds

handful of flat leaf parsley, finely
   chopped
sea salt and pepper
To serve
200g (7oz) roasted cherry tomatoes
   (page 54)

1 Trim the fennel bulbs, reserving the feathery fronds and discarding the
stalks and tough outer layers. Slice the bulbs thinly, then chop finely. Chop
the feathery tops as well; set aside.
2 Heat the olive oil in a large pan, add the chopped fennel and cook over a
low heat for 10 minutes. Add the broth, fennel seeds and seasoning. Bring to
the boil and simmer for 30 minutes.
3 Stir in the chopped parsley and ladle the soup into warm bowls. Top with
the roasted cherry tomatoes and fennel fronds to serve.

In the high bleak mountains of Sardinia, small
wild fennel bulbs grow everywhere and they
are a popular ingredient in local dishes.
Cultivated fennel works perfectly well here.

Livorno fish soup

Illustrated on previous pages

Serves 6

4 tbsp olive oil

1 onion, peeled and finely chopped

1 carrot, peeled and finely chopped

1 celery stalk, finely chopped

handful of flat leaf parsley, chopped

small piece of hot red chilli, very
   finely chopped

500g (1lb 2oz) raw prawns in shell

2 medium squid, cleaned and sliced
   into rings

250ml (8fl oz) dry white wine

300g (11oz) plum tomatoes, skinned
   and chopped

500g (1lb 2oz) fresh mussels, cleaned

500g (1lb 2oz) fresh clams, cleaned

650g (1lb 7oz) sea bream, filleted
   and skinned

1 small cooked lobster, cleaned
   (optional)

sea salt and pepper

To serve

6 thin slices of firm, coarse-textured
   bread

2 garlic cloves, peeled and crushed

1 Heat the olive oil in a large pan, add the onion, carrot, celery, parsley and chilli, and cook over a medium heat until the onion begins to colour. Stir in the prawns and squid and cook gently for 10 minutes, then remove the prawns and set aside. Add the wine, 125ml (4fl oz) hot water and the tomatoes and simmer for a further 10 minutes. Season with salt. Remove the squid and set aside.

2 Put the mussels and clams into a steamer over boiling water, cover tightly and steam the shellfish just until they open, about 3–5 minutes. Discard any that remain closed.

3 Meanwhile, strain the vegetables and cooking liquor through a fine sieve into a saucepan, rubbing with the back of a ladle. Add the bream fillets and simmer until opaque, about 4–5 minutes. Add all the seafood to the pan, including the lobster if using. Heat through gently and check the seasoning. In the meantime, toast the bread slices and spread with the garlic. Place in warm soup bowls, ladle the fish soup over the garlic toasts and serve.

Livorno is a city by the sea in Tuscany, famous for its beautiful 17th century port. It is also renowned for its robust fish soup or stew, which is made from a variety of Mediterranean fish and shellfish.

Chicken soup with poached egg

Serves 6

1.5 litres (2½ pints) chicken broth (page 64)
1 bay leaf
6 thin slices of day-old, coarse-textured bread
6 eggs
sea salt and pepper

To serve

handful of flat leaf parsley, finely chopped
50g (2oz) Parmesan cheese, freshly grated
freshly grated nutmeg, to taste

1 Heat the chicken broth in a large, wide pan. Add the bay leaf and simmer gently over a medium heat for 10 minutes, then discard the bay leaf and check the seasoning. In the meantime, toast the bread slices.

2 One at a time, break the eggs into a cup and gently pour into the hot broth. The egg whites will immediately coagulate. Continue to poach until the whites are set.

3 Put a slice of toasted bread into each warm soup bowl. Using a slotted spoon, carefully place a poached egg on top, then ladle in the fragrant broth. Scatter the parsley and Parmesan on top and sprinkle with a little grated nutmeg. Serve at once.

Known as zuppa alla pavese, this dish comes from Padua. It is perfect for a cold winter's evening – substantial, interesting and very tasty. A good homemade broth is essential.

Lentil soup with pancetta and potatoes

Serves 6

10 new potatoes, preferably Italian,
  scrubbed
3 bay leaves
100g (3½oz) pancetta, diced
2 garlic cloves, peeled and crushed
225g (8oz) small green lentils
3 tbsp olive oil
700g jar tomato passata, or 2 x 400g
  cans chopped tomatoes
sea salt and pepper

To serve

50g (2oz) Parmesan cheese, freshly
  grated
generous handful of flat leaf parsley,
  chopped
extra virgin olive oil, to drizzle

1 Cut the potatoes into even-sized cubes and put into a medium saucepan.
Pour in 900ml (1½ pints) boiling water and add the bay leaves, salt and
pepper. Bring to a simmer and cook for 10 minutes.

2 In the meantime, fry the pancetta dice in a dry frying pan over a medium
heat, turning frequently, until golden.

3 Add the pancetta to the potatoes, with the garlic, lentils, olive oil, passata
or chopped tomatoes and some pepper. Return to a simmer, cover and cook
for 40 minutes. Adjust the seasoning.

4 Serve sprinkled with Parmesan and parsley, and topped with a generous
drizzle of good, fruity extra virgin olive oil.

For this tasty soup, use Castelluccio lentils
from Italy if possible, otherwise the French
Puy lentils are an acceptable alternative.

Potato and sausage soup

Serves 6

1.5 litres (2½ pints) chicken broth (page 64)

3 medium potatoes, peeled and sliced

1 onion, peeled and finely chopped

125ml (4 fl oz) milk

1 tbsp semolina

2 cooked Italian sausages, thinly sliced

sea salt and pepper

To serve

handful of flat leaf parsley, finely chopped

freshly grated Parmesan cheese, to taste

1 Heat the chicken broth in a large saucepan, then add the sliced potatoes and chopped onion. Cook over a medium heat for 10–15 minutes or until the potato is soft.

2 Using a slotted spoon, remove the potato and onion from the stock and pass through a food mill, or mash until smooth, then return to the liquid.

3 Add the milk and sprinkle the semolina over the soup, stirring constantly. Cook over a medium heat, stirring, for 10 minutes. Add the sausage slices and cook for a further 10 minutes. Season with salt and pepper to taste.

4 Ladle the soup into warm bowls and scatter over the parsley. Sprinkle with Parmesan and serve.

This comforting, hearty soup comes from Emilia-Romagna, the gastronomic centre of Italy. You can vary the flavour by using different types of sausages. Freshly grated Parmesan and plenty of parsley are essential.

easy
breads
and pizzas

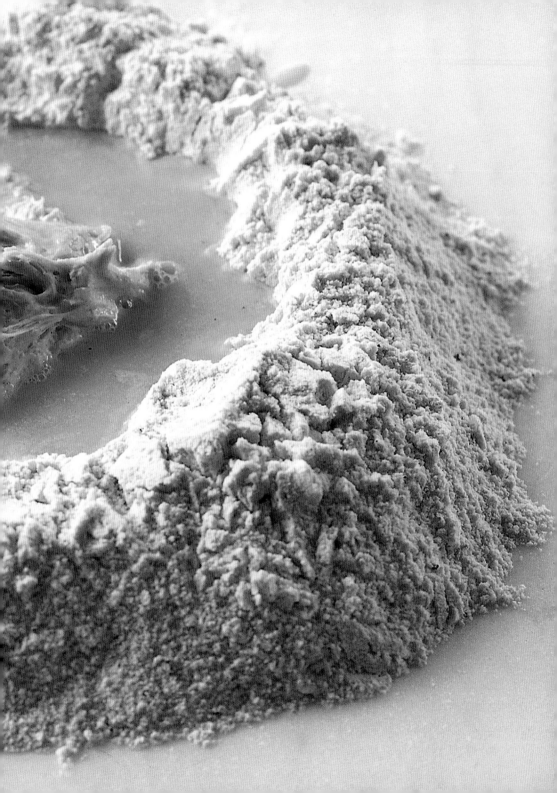

Ciabatta

Makes 4 loaves

7g (¼oz) fresh yeast, or 1 tsp fast-
action dried yeast

500g (1lb 2oz) strong white bread
flour

15g (½oz) sea salt

500g (1lb 2oz) biga (see right)

olive oil, to oil

1 Measure 300ml (½ pint) warm water in a jug. In a small bowl, blend the
fresh yeast (or simply mix the dried yeast) with 3 tbsp of this water.
2 Combine the flour and salt in a large bowl, make a well in the centre and
add the biga, yeast liquid and water. Mix together to form a sticky dough,
then knead well to develop the elasticity. As it is wet, the dough will
continually adhere to your hand in large elastic lumps, but persevere, or use
a mixer to knead it if you prefer. Do the stretch test (see below) to check the
dough is ready.
3 Liberally oil a large bowl, drop in the dough and turn it carefully to bathe
in olive oil. Leave in a warm place until doubled or even trebled in volume,
1½–2 hours or possibly even longer.
4 Oil two baking trays. Gently ease the puffy dough on to a well-floured
surface, avoiding knocking it down. With floured hands and a dough scraper
or sharp knife, cut into 4 pieces. As you pick each piece up, gently roll in
the flour and give it a hearty stretch to elongate it to the classic slipper
shape, then place on the baking trays. Cover and leave to prove for an hour.
5 Meanwhile, preheat the oven to 200°C (fan oven 180°C), gas mark 6. After
proving the loaves will still look flat, but they will spring up in the oven.
Bake them for 20 minutes until golden. Cool on a wire rack and eat warm.

stretch test To check whether a dough has been kneaded enough for the
gluten to develop elasticity, stretch a piece of dough between your fingers. It
should behave like an elastic band, not ripping or breaking. This is what I
call 'the stretch test', vital when making breads.

Enriched with olive oil, crisp and flavourful,
this is the bread that all bakers aspire to
make, yet it really is quite simple.

Biga

Makes about 1kg (2¼lb)
7g (¼oz) fresh yeast, or 1 tsp fast-
   action dried yeast
575g (1¼lb) strong white bread flour

1 Measure 400ml (14fl oz) warm water in a jug. In a small bowl, blend the
fresh yeast (or simply mix dried yeast) with a little of this water.
2 Mix all the biga ingredients together in a large bowl and beat with a spoon
or your hands until you have a smooth, loose dough. You should feel the
elasticity as the gluten develops. Cover and leave to stand at room
temperature for 12–24 hours.

This fermented yeast starter is the basis for
many Italian breads. It enhances the function
of the yeast in the dough, helps develop that
yeasty aroma and gives a characteristic open
texture. Use fresh yeast if possible. You won't
need all the biga for the ciabatta or any of my
other breads but you can keep the rest in the
fridge for up to 3 days – for another loaf.

Olive and rosemary focaccia

Illustrated on previous pages

Makes 1 large loaf

2 large rosemary sprigs
2 tbsp olive oil
1 onion, peeled, halved and sliced
2 garlic cloves, peeled and finely
  chopped
10 black olives, pitted and halved
  lengthways
sea salt and coarsely ground pepper

For the dough

7g (¼oz) fresh yeast, or 1 tsp fast-
  action dried yeast
275g (10oz) strong white flour
1 tsp sea salt
25g (1oz) wholemeal flour
100g (3½oz) biga (page 93)
olive oil, to oil

1 Finely chop a third of the rosemary leaves; keep another third whole; break the rest into tiny sprigs and set aside for the topping. Heat the olive oil in a frying pan and sauté the onion and chopped rosemary for 10 minutes. Add the garlic and cook until the mixture caramelises. Tip into a bowl and cool.
2 For the dough, dissolve the yeast in 225ml (7½fl oz) warm water. Mix the white flour with the sea salt on the work surface, pile into a mound and make a well in the centre. Add the wholemeal flour, biga and yeast liquid to the well, then gradually draw in the white flour with your hands and mix to a dough, adding a little extra water if necessary.

3 Knead the dough for 10 minutes until smooth and elastic, then add half the caramelised onion and continue to knead for 10 minutes. Do the stretch test to check that the dough is ready (see page 92). Place in a lightly oiled large bowl and turn the dough to coat. Cover with a tea towel and leave in a warm place for 2 hours or until almost doubled in bulk.

4 Tip the dough out on to a lightly floured surface and gently knead into a round ball. Place on a well oiled large baking tray. Cover and allow to rest for 15 minutes, then flatten the dough with the palm of your hand to a 20cm (8 inch) round.

5 Mix the rosemary leaves with the remaining onion mixture and spread evenly over the surface of the dough. Season generously with pepper. Cover to prevent a skin forming and leave to prove for 2 hours.

6 Preheat the oven to 200°C (fan oven 180°C), gas mark 6. Stud the dough with the olives and scatter with sea salt. Bake for 15–18 minutes until golden. Transfer to a wire rack to cool slightly and serve warm, scattered with rosemary sprigs.

Flavoured with caramelised onion and garlic, and topped with olives, sea salt and rosemary before baking, this classic bread is best served warm, drizzled with new season's olive oil.

Honey bread

Also illustrated on previous pages

Makes 1 large loaf

15g (½oz) fresh yeast, or 2 tsp fast-action dried yeast

275ml (9fl oz) warm whole milk

175ml (6fl oz) thin honey

2 tbsp melted unsalted butter, cooled

2 tbsp olive oil, plus extra to oil

1 large egg, beaten

1½ tsp sea salt

2 tbsp aniseed seeds

1 tbsp finely grated unwaxed lemon zest

450g (1lb) strong white flour, plus extra if needed

For the filling and topping

50g (2oz) raisins

50g (2oz) shelled walnuts, finely chopped

50g (2oz) pitted prunes, finely chopped

3 tbsp thin honey

1 Dissolve the yeast in 125ml (4fl oz) warm water in a large bowl, then leave for 10 minutes.

2 Add the milk, 175ml (6fl oz) honey, the melted butter, olive oil, egg, salt, aniseed and lemon zest to the yeast liquid and stir well.

3 Add the flour and mix with your hands to obtain a ball of dough. If the dough is sticky, mix in a little extra flour. Knead well for 10 minutes to form a soft, smooth, elastic dough. Do the stretch test (see page 92) to check that it is ready. Cover and leave to rise for 1½ hours or until doubled in size.

4 In a small bowl, mix together the raisins, walnuts and prunes. Punch back the dough and turn it out on to a lightly floured surface. Knead for 2–3 minutes, then roll out to a 40cm (16 inch) round. Using a brush, spread 2 tbsp of the honey over the dough and sprinkle with three-quarters of the fruit and nut mixture.

5 Roll the dough up to enclose the filling and form a 40cm (16 inch) long loaf, about 7.5cm (3 inches) thick. Press the ends together to seal, or the honey will seep out. Lift on to a lightly oiled baking tray, cover and set aside to prove for 40–60 minutes.

6 Meanwhile, preheat the oven to 200°C (fan oven 180°C), gas mark 6. Bake the loaf for 30 minutes until the crust is golden brown. Transfer to a wire rack and brush with the remaining honey, then sprinkle the rest of the nut and fruit mixture on top. Cool before serving. This enriched sweet bread will keep for a day or two. It is also delicious toasted.

Semolina bread rolls

Illustrated on previous pages

Makes 12 rolls
7g (¼oz) fresh yeast, or 1 tsp fast-
    action dried yeast
375g (13oz) strong white flour
275g (10oz) semolina

2 tsp coarsely ground black pepper
125g (4oz) biga (page 93)
15g (½oz) sea salt
olive oil, to oil
2 tbsp coarse sea salt, to sprinkle

1 Dissolve the yeast in 375ml (13fl oz) warm water. Combine the flour, semolina and black pepper on a work surface and pile into a mound. Make a well in the centre and add the yeast water and biga. Mix with your hands until all the ingredients are well combined – this will take about 5 minutes.
2 Add the sea salt and knead the dough for 10 minutes until smooth and elastic. Do the stretch test to check that the dough is ready (see page 92). Place the dough in a lightly oiled large bowl, cover with cling film and leave in a warm place until doubled in size, approximately 2 hours.
3 Knock back the dough in the bowl, re-cover and leave to rise again for 45 minutes. This second rising will give the dough more strength.
4 Tip the dough on to a lightly floured surface and cut into 12 pieces, using a dough scraper or sharp knife. Shape into balls, place on a lightly oiled baking tray and leave to prove for another hour.
5 Preheat the oven to 200°C (fan oven 180°C), gas mark 6. Using a sharp knife, cut a cross on top of each roll, then sprinkle liberally with coarse salt. Bake for 20 minutes, opening the oven door slightly for the last 5 minutes – this makes the rolls crisper. Cool on a wire rack and eat warm.

These rolls are from Puglia in southern Italy. Semolina imparts colour and a slightly grainy texture and crust. Flavour the dough with a handful of chopped fresh herbs (or sprinkling of dried) if you like. Ideal breakfast rolls, they are also great for panini (pages 109–110).

Mozzarella and baby spinach ciabatta

Serves 2

½ ciabatta loaf
extra virgin olive oil, to drizzle
large handful of baby spinach leaves
12 black olives, pitted
4 thin slices of red onion

4 generous slices of buffalo
  mozzarella cheese
6 canned anchovy fillets in oil,
  drained
sea salt and pepper

1 Cut the ciabatta into two portions, then split each horizontally. Moisten the insides with extra virgin olive oil.

2 Lay a few baby spinach leaves on each ciabatta base and scatter over the olives and red onion. Lay the mozzarella slices on top and add the anchovy fillets. Cover with another layer of spinach and season with salt and pepper.

3 Put the ciabatta 'lids' on top of the filling and press down lightly. Warm in the oven to serve if required.

In Italy, bread plays a part in virtually every meal. Ciabatta loaves are great for Italian sandwiches or 'panini', but you can also use sfilatino or focaccia, or homemade breads.

Taleggio, artichoke and rocket ciabatta

Serves 4–5

1 ciabatta loaf
extra virgin olive oil, to drizzle
250g (9oz) Taleggio cheese, thinly
  sliced

2 large handfuls of baby rocket
  leaves
150g (5oz) drained artichoke hearts
  preserved in oil
sea salt and pepper

1 Split the ciabatta loaf in half horizontally and drizzle the cut surfaces with extra virgin olive oil.

2 Layer the Taleggio cheese slices on the base and top with the rocket leaves. Slice the artichoke hearts and arrange on top of the rocket leaves. Season lightly with salt and generously with pepper.

3 Position the top of the loaf and press down lightly. Warm through in the oven if required. Cut into sections to serve.

Cherry tomato, speck and cheese panini

Serves 1
1 ciabatta roll
extra virgin olive oil, to drizzle
4 cherry tomatoes, halved
4 thin slices of red onion

2 slices speck (smoked, salt-cured,
  air-dried ham)
3 slices of smoked scamorza or
  mozzarella cheese
sea salt and pepper

1 Split the ciabatta roll in half and moisten the insides with extra virgin olive oil.
2 Place the halved cherry tomatoes on the base and top with the red onion slices. Cover with the speck slices. Arrange the scamorza or mozzarella slices on top and season generously with pepper, but lightly with salt.
3 Position the top of the roll, press down lightly and warm in the oven to serve if preferred.

'Panino' literally means a bread roll, but nowadays it usually refers to a filled roll. An Italian 'panino' is a truly wonderful marriage of tasty filling ingredients and crisp, crusty bread. It is either eaten cold or hot – after warming in a salamander or low oven.

Prosciutto and roasted pepper panini

Serves 1

1 ciabatta roll
extra virgin olive oil, to drizzle
2–3 radicchio leaves, torn
2 thin slices of fontina cheese

small handful of wild rocket leaves
3–4 slices of roasted red pepper
  (from the deli counter)
2 thin slices prosciutto
sea salt and pepper

1 Split the ciabatta roll in half and moisten the cut surfaces with extra virgin olive oil.

2 Layer the radicchio leaves and fontina cheese slices on the base and add some wild rocket leaves and roasted red pepper slices. Loosely fold the prosciutto slices and arrange on top.

3 Season generously with salt and pepper. Position the top of the roll and press down lightly. Heat through to serve if preferred.

A 'panino' makes a very satisfying fast lunch, though in Italy it might be eaten instead of breakfast, or as a mid-morning brunch.

Pizza dough base

Makes two 25cm (10 inch) bases

15g (½oz) fresh yeast, or 1½ tsp fast-action dried yeast

250g (9oz) strong white unbleached flour

½ tsp sea salt

50ml (2fl oz) olive oil, plus extra to oil

semolina, to sprinkle

1 Measure 50ml (2fl oz) warm water in a jug. Blend the fresh yeast (or simply mix dried yeast) with a little of this water.

2 Sift the flour and salt together into a large bowl. Make a well in the centre and add the olive oil, yeast liquid and some of the water. Mix together with a wooden spoon, gradually adding the remaining water, to form a soft dough.

3 Turn the dough out on to a lightly floured surface and knead vigorously for 10 minutes until it is soft and satiny (don't be afraid of adding more flour). Place in a lightly oiled large bowl, then turn the dough around to coat with the oil. Cover the bowl with a clean tea towel and leave in a warm place for 1½ hours or until the dough has doubled in size.

4 Preheat the oven to 200°C (fan oven 180°C), gas mark 6. In the bottom of the oven, preheat two oiled baking sheets or a terracotta pizza stone. Knock down the dough with your knuckles, then knead on a lightly floured surface for 2–3 minutes to knock out the air bubbles. Divide the dough in half.

5 On a lightly floured surface, preferably marble, roll out the pieces of dough very, very thinly, until 25–30cm (10–12 inches) in diameter. (They should be as thin as a paper napkin folded in four.) Now lift each pizza base on to a cold baking sheet sprinkled generously with semolina (this will make it easier to slide the pizza off). Add your chosen topping.

6 Lightly oil the preheated baking sheets. Carefully slide the prepared pizzas off the cold baking sheets directly on to the hot baking sheets or pizza stone and immediately bake in the oven for 20–25 minutes until golden and crisp.

Pizzas were first created in Naples and the best pizzas are still made in the south, where local wheat and water produce a fine texture and crust. The best type of flour to use is Italian '0' grade ('00' pasta flour isn't suitable).

Pizza marinara

Serves 2

1 quantity pizza dough (page 112)
semolina, to sprinkle
4–5 fresh plum tomatoes, skinned
6–8 basil leaves, torn

1 garlic clove, peeled and chopped
3 tsp dried oregano
sea salt and pepper
olive oil, to oil
extra virgin olive oil, to drizzle

1 Preheat the oven to 200°C (fan oven 180°C), gas mark 6, and preheat two baking sheets or a pizza stone. On a lightly floured surface, roll out the pizza dough very thinly into two 25–30cm (10–12 inch) rounds, then lift each pizza base on to a cold baking sheet sprinkled with semolina (see page 112).

2 Put the tomatoes, basil and seasoning in a blender or food processor and whiz to a purée, or pass through a food mill. Spread this tomato sauce over the pizza bases and top with the garlic and oregano.

3 Lightly oil the hot baking sheets and slide the pizzas on to them. Bake for about 20 minutes until the crust is crisp and golden brown. Drizzle with extra virgin olive oil to serve.

This is the original, simple tomato pizza, one of only two authentic pizzas according to purists in Naples (the margarita is the other.) I favour the marinara because I love its fresh taste and simplicity. For extra flavour, scatter some anchovies on top before baking.

Pizza with aubergine and ricotta

Illustrated on previous pages

Serves 2

1 quantity pizza dough (page 112)
1 medium aubergine
3 tbsp olive oil, plus extra to oil
1 small red onion, peeled and sliced
  into rings
4 ripe tomatoes, skinned and sliced

semolina, to sprinkle
25g (1oz) Parmesan cheese, freshly
  grated
250g (9oz) ricotta cheese
good handful of basil leaves
sea salt and pepper

1 Wrap the pizza dough in cling film and set aside until you are ready to roll out. Slice the aubergine lengthways, then put the slices into a colander, sprinkle with salt, cover and weight down. Leave for 30 minutes to degorge the bitter juices.

2 Preheat the oven to 200°C (fan oven 180°C), gas mark 6, and preheat two baking sheets or a pizza stone. Preheat the grill to medium.

3 Heat a third of the olive oil in a saucepan, add the onion rings and fry until softened. Add the tomatoes, salt and pepper and set aside.

4 Rinse the aubergines to remove the salt and pat dry. Brush the aubergine slices with half the remaining olive oil and grill for 5 minutes on each side until lightly cooked.

5 On a lightly floured surface, roll out the pizza dough very thinly into two 25–30cm (10–12 inch) rounds. Now lift each pizza base on to a cold baking sheet sprinkled with semolina (see page 112). Brush with the remaining olive oil, then spread with the tomato mixture. Sprinkle over the Parmesan cheese and add the ricotta. Arrange the aubergine slices on top, radiating from the centre, then tuck some of the basil leaves under the slices.

6 Lightly oil the hot baking sheets and slide the pizzas on to them. Bake for 20–25 minutes until golden and bubbling. Serve hot, scattered with the rest of the basil leaves.

Pizza norcina

Serves 2

1 quantity pizza dough (page 112)
25g (1oz) dried porcini mushrooms
250g (9oz) large flat mushrooms, wiped
2 tbsp olive oil, plus extra to oil

1 garlic clove, peeled and crushed
semolina, to sprinkle
250g (9oz) mozzarella cheese, grated
25g (1oz) truffle paste (salsina)
sea salt and pepper

1 Wrap the pizza dough in cling film and set aside until ready to roll out. Preheat the oven to 200°C (fan oven 180°C), gas mark 6, and preheat two baking sheets or a pizza stone.

2 Soak the dried porcini in warm water to cover for about 20 minutes, then drain and pat dry. Slice the fresh mushrooms.

3 Heat the olive oil in a frying pan, add the porcini and fresh mushrooms and fry until softened. Add the garlic and some salt and pepper.

4 On a lightly floured surface, roll out the pizza dough very thinly into two 25–30cm (10–12 inch) rounds. Now lift each pizza base on to a cold baking sheet sprinkled with semolina (see page 112). Top the pizza bases with the mushrooms and mozzarella, then add little mounds of truffle paste.

5 Lightly oil the hot baking sheets and slide the pizzas on to them. Bake for 20–25 minutes until golden and bubbling. Serve immediately.

I first enjoyed this pizza in Norcina, in Umbria, a region famous for its truffles. Here I've used truffle paste, which is made from a combination of truffle and porcini mushrooms. It is available in jars.

Pizza Margarita

Serves 4–6
1 quantity pizza dough (page 112)
semolina, to sprinkle
large handful of basil leaves, torn
675g (1½lb) cherry tomatoes, halved
small handful of oregano leaves,
  chopped
250g (9oz) mozzarella cheese, grated
olive oil, to oil
sea salt and pepper

1 Preheat the oven to 200°C (fan oven 180°C), gas mark 6, and preheat two
baking sheets or a pizza stone. On a lightly floured surface, roll out the
dough very thinly into two 25–30cm (10–12 inch) rounds. Now lift each
pizza base on to a cold baking sheet sprinkled with semolina (see page 112).
2 Scatter the basil leaves over the pizza bases, then add the cherry tomato
halves, chopped oregano, salt, pepper and grated mozzarella.
3 Lightly oil the hot baking sheets and slide the pizzas on to them. Bake for
about 20 minutes until the cherry tomatoes are softened and the cheese is
bubbling and golden.

This tomato and mozzarella pizza couldn't be
more simple. For the best flavour, choose
bright red, ripe tomatoes with a distinctive
peppery aroma (detected at the stalk end).

Asparagus calzone

Illustrated on previous pages

Serves 2

1 quantity pizza dough (page 112)
2 tender, young courgettes
300g (11oz) asparagus spears
150g (5oz) ricotta cheese

1 tbsp freshly grated Parmesan
  cheese
2 tbsp olive oil, plus extra to oil
semolina, to sprinkle
sea salt and pepper

1 Wrap the pizza dough in cling film and set aside until ready to roll out. Preheat the oven to 200°C (fan oven 180°C), gas mark 6, and preheat a baking sheet or a pizza stone. Slice the courgettes, place in a colander and sprinkle with salt. Leave for 20 minutes, then rinse under cold water and pat dry.

2 Cut off the pale stalk ends and peel the lower end of the asparagus stalks, using a swivel vegetable peeler. Add the asparagus spears to a saucepan of boiling water, bring back to the boil, then immediately drain and rinse under cold water. Cut into 5cm (2 inch) pieces and pat dry.

3 Put the asparagus, courgettes, ricotta and Parmesan into a bowl. Mix together and season with salt and pepper to taste. Stir in 1 tbsp olive oil.

4 On a lightly floured surface, roll out the pizza dough into two 25–30cm (10–12 inch) rounds. Now lift each round on to a cold baking sheet sprinkled with semolina (see page 112). Pile the filling on one side of each round, moisten the edge with water and bring the uncovered side over the filling. Using your fingers, press the edges together to seal, fold them up and crimp.

5 Brush the calzone with the remaining olive oil. Lightly oil the hot baking sheet and slide the calzone on to them. Bake for 20–25 minutes until golden brown. Allow to stand for 10 minutes before serving.

To make calzone, you simply fold the pizza dough over the filling and seal the edges, like a pasty. Here, the sweet, succulent flavour and aroma of fresh asparagus is held within, until you cut into the calzone. Make this in early summer, when young, homegrown asparagus is in season.

Gorgonzola and artichoke pizza

Serves 2

1 quantity pizza dough (page 112)
6 canned artichoke hearts
3 tbsp olive oil, plus extra to oil
semolina, to sprinkle
150g (5 oz) mozzarella cheese, grated

150g (5 oz) Gorgonzola cheese, sliced
3 tbsp Parmesan cheese, freshly
  grated
1 tbsp pine nuts, toasted
1 tsp finely chopped sage
sea salt and pepper

1 Wrap the pizza dough in cling film and set aside until ready to roll out. Preheat the oven to 200°C (fan oven 180°C), gas mark 6, and preheat two baking sheets or a pizza stone.

2 Rinse the artichokes well, pat dry and place in a small roasting tin. Drizzle with the olive oil and roast in the oven for 10 minutes until golden. Transfer to a board and cut into quarters.

3 On a lightly floured surface, roll out the pizza dough very thinly into two 25–30cm (10–12 inch) rounds. Now lift each pizza base on to a cold baking sheet sprinkled with semolina (see page 112).

4 Scatter the mozzarella and Gorgonzola on top of the pizza bases and arrange the artichoke hearts on top. Sprinkle over the Parmesan, pine nuts and sage, and season with salt and pepper.

5 Lightly oil the hot baking sheets and slide the pizzas on to them. Bake for 20–25 minutes until golden and bubbling. Eat hot or cold.

This versatile pizza can be served hot straight from the oven, or eaten cold on a picnic.

Spinach, olive and onion testo

Makes 1

For the dough

15g (½oz) fresh yeast, or 1½ tsp fast action dried yeast

500g (1lb 2oz) strong white unbleached flour

2 tsp sea salt

3 tbsp olive oil

For the filling

2 tbsp olive oil, plus extra to oil

1 large red onion, peeled and sliced

1 garlic clove, peeled and crushed

½ dried long, thin red chilli (peperoncini), crushed

750g (1lb 10oz) spinach, trimmed, washed and finely chopped

125g (4oz) pitted green olives

75g (3oz) mozzarella cheese, diced

sea salt and pepper

To finish

olive oil, to drizzle

coarse sea salt, to sprinkle

1 First prepare the dough. Measure 275ml (9fl oz) warm water in a jug. Mix the yeast with 1 tbsp of the water. Put the flour and salt into a large bowl and mix well together. Make a well in the middle and pour in the yeast liquid, the olive oil and some of the remaining water. Mix together, gradually adding the rest of the measured water, to form a soft dough.

2 Turn the dough on to a lightly floured work surface and knead vigorously for 10 minutes until smooth. Return the dough to a clean bowl, cover with a cloth and leave in a warm place for 45 minutes until doubled in size.

3 Knead the risen dough again for 1–2 minutes to knock out the air bubbles. Return to the bowl, cover and leave to rise for about 40 minutes.

4 For the filling, heat the olive oil in a large frying pan. Add the onion, garlic and chilli, and cook for about 5 minutes. Add the spinach and cook for another 5 minutes until it is wilted. Take off the heat, add the olives and season with salt and pepper. Allow to cool, then mix in the mozzarella.

5 Divide the dough in half. Roll out each piece on a lightly floured surface to a 33cm (13 inch) round. Place one round on a lightly oiled baking sheet and spoon the filling on top, leaving a margin around the edge. Dampen the edge, cover with the second round of dough and pinch the edges together to seal. Leave to prove for 30 minutes.

6 Preheat the oven to 200°C (fan oven 180°C), gas mark 6. Drizzle the testo with olive oil and sprinkle with salt. Bake for 25 minutes, then transfer to a wire rack to cool. Serve hot, warm or cold, cut into wedges.

easy pasta, polenta and rice

Parsley pasta with clams and black olives

Serves 4

350g (12oz) dried linguine or
  trenette pasta
very large handful of flat leaf
  parsley, finely chopped
3 tbsp extra virgin olive oil
sea salt and pepper

For the clam sauce

10 ripe plum tomatoes
2 tbsp olive oil
3 garlic cloves, peeled and chopped
40 fresh clams
1 celery stalk, very finely chopped
20 Gaeta olives, pitted
175ml (6fl oz) dry white wine
handful of basil leaves, roughly torn

1 For the sauce, immerse the tomatoes in a bowl of boiling hot water for
10 seconds to loosen the skins, then drain and peel away the skins. Chop the
tomato flesh. Heat the olive oil in a large heavy-based sauté pan. Add the
garlic and sauté over a medium heat until very lightly golden. Add the
clams, cover the pan with a tight-fitting lid and cook over a high heat for
4–6 minutes until the shells have opened. Discard any that remain closed.
2 Meanwhile, add the pasta to a large pan of boiling salted water and cook at
a fast boil until al dente (tender but firm to the bite).
3 Add the tomatoes, celery, olives and wine to the clams and cook until the
wine evaporates, about 1 minute. Season with salt and pepper to taste and
scatter in the torn basil. Take off the heat.
4 Drain the pasta well and toss with the parsley and extra virgin olive oil.
Combine with the clam sauce, and eat straightaway.

Fine pasta, such as linguine and trenette, is
superb with a clam and olive sauce. The small,
sweet Venus clams are my favourite.

Pasta 'Norma'

Serves 6

1kg (2¼lb) fresh plum tomatoes, or
  2 x 400g cans chopped tomatoes
5 tbsp olive oil
1 onion, peeled and finely chopped
2 garlic cloves, peeled and crushed
2 medium aubergines, trimmed

450–500g (1lb–1lb 2oz) penne rigate
  (quills with ridges)
handful of small basil leaves
sea salt and pepper
freshly grated Parmesan cheese,
  to serve

1 If using fresh tomatoes, plunge them into boiling water for 10 seconds, then drain and peel away the skins. Quarter the tomatoes and remove the cores. Heat 2 tbsp olive oil in a large saucepan, add the onion and sauté for a few minutes to soften. Add the crushed garlic and sauté for a minute or two, then add the prepared fresh or canned tomatoes and season well with salt and pepper. Cover and cook for 25 minutes.

2 Meanwhile, slice the aubergines lengthways into strips, 2cm (¾ inch) long. Sprinkle with salt, place in a bowl or colander and weight down. Leave to degorge their bitter juices for 20 minutes. Rinse the aubergine strips thoroughly and pat dry.

3 Heat the remaining olive oil in a large frying pan, add the aubergine strips and fry for about 10 minutes, turning frequently, until golden brown on all sides and tender. Drain on kitchen paper.

4 Bring a large saucepan of salted water to the boil. Add the pasta and cook in fast boiling water until al dente (tender but firm to the bite). Drain the pasta and toss with the tomato sauce and aubergine. Scatter with the basil leaves and serve, with plenty of grated Parmesan.

This is a typical southern Italian pasta dish –
colourful, with robust flavours. When fresh
plum tomatoes are out of season, use canned
tomatoes – flavoured with herbs if you like.

Tagliatelle with garlic prawns and tomato

Illustrated on previous pages

Serves 4

350g (12oz) dried tagliatelle
3 tbsp olive oil
225g (8oz) raw tiger prawns, peeled
  and deveined
2 garlic cloves, peeled and crushed

1 red chilli, deseeded and chopped
8 plum tomatoes, halved, deseeded
  and finely chopped
2 tbsp roughly torn flat leaf parsley
sea salt and pepper

1 Bring a large saucepan of salted water to the boil. Add the pasta and cook in fast boiling water until al dente (tender but firm to the bite).
2 Meanwhile, heat the olive oil in a sauté pan. Add the prawns with the crushed garlic and chopped chilli, and sauté for 3–4 minutes or until the prawns turn pink. Add the chopped plum tomatoes and parsley, and toss to mix. Season with salt and pepper to taste.
3 When the pasta is cooked, drain and divide between warm bowls. Spoon on the prawn and tomato sauce, and serve.

It is almost impossible to imagine Italian food without tomatoes. Make sure you select full-flavoured tomatoes – firm, red and with a good fruity scent.

Pasta with creamy three cheese sauce

Serves 4

350g (12oz) dried fusilli or pasta shells

125g (4oz) ricotta cheese

125g (4oz) dolcelatte cheese, cut into cubes

125g (4oz) Taleggio cheese, cut into cubes

4 tbsp chopped flat leaf parsley

sea salt and pepper

freshly grated Parmesan cheese, to serve

1 Bring a large saucepan of salted water to the boil. Add the pasta and cook in fast boiling water until al dente (tender but firm to the bite).

2 Drain the pasta and return to the pan. Add the three cheeses and toss until melted into an instant creamy sauce.

3 Divide between warm bowls, scatter with the chopped parsley, grated Parmesan and a generous grinding of black pepper. Serve straightaway.

Soft cheeses melt effortlessly as they are tossed with hot pasta, to make a deliciously rich creamy sauce.

Pasta with pancetta and tomato sauce

Serves 4

1 tbsp olive oil

125g (4oz) pancetta, diced

2 garlic cloves, peeled and crushed

8 plum tomatoes, halved, deseeded and chopped

handful of sage leaves, chopped

350g (12oz) dried bucatini or spaghetti

2 tbsp chopped flat leaf parsley

sea salt and pepper

freshly grated Parmesan cheese, to serve

1 Heat the olive oil in a pan, add the pancetta and fry until it is cooked and crisp. Add the garlic, chopped tomatoes and sage. Cook gently for 6 minutes.

2 Meanwhile, add the pasta to a large pan of boiling salted water and cook at a fast boil until al dente (tender but firm to the bite).

3 Drain the pasta and toss with the pancetta and tomato sauce. Season with salt and pepper to taste.

4 Divide between warm bowls and scatter over the chopped parsley. Serve with plenty of freshly grated Parmesan.

Pancetta is the Italian equivalent of our streaky bacon, but much more flavoursome. It makes a great base for tasty pasta sauces and is conveniently sold ready diced in packets, as well as in slices and by the piece.

Spaghetti carbonara

Serves 4
1 tbsp olive oil
125g (4oz) pancetta, diced
1 finely chopped garlic clove
350g (12oz) dried spaghetti
2 very fresh large eggs

142ml carton single cream
2 tbsp freshly grated Parmesan
  cheese
sea salt and pepper
extra freshly grated Parmesan
  cheese, to serve

1 Heat the olive oil in a pan, add the pancetta and garlic and fry until the
pancetta is cooked and crisp; leave to cool.
2 Bring a large saucepan of salted water to the boil. Add the spaghetti and
cook in fast boiling water until al dente (tender but firm to the bite).
3 For the carbonara sauce, beat the eggs, cream and Parmesan together in a
bowl, then add the pancetta with the pan juices.
4 Drain the cooked spaghetti, return to the pan and immediately pour in the
carbonara sauce. Toss to coat and allow the egg to 'set' slightly.
5 Divide between warm bowls and sprinkle with freshly ground pepper.
Serve with lots more Parmesan.

In this classic recipe, the heat of the pasta
effectively cooks the egg as you toss the hot
spaghetti with the creamy sauce. Pancetta
lends a special flavour.

Pasta with tomato and chilli sauce

Serves 4

2 tbsp olive oil

4 garlic cloves, peeled and finely chopped

250g (9oz) baby plum tomatoes

1–2 red chillies, deseeded and chopped

350g (12oz) dried penne or other pasta

2 tbsp torn basil leaves

2 tbsp chopped flat leaf parsley

sea salt and pepper

Parmesan cheese shavings, to serve

1 Heat the olive oil in a pan, add the garlic and fry gently until softened. Add the baby plum tomatoes and fresh chilli to taste. Cook over a gentle heat for about 15 minutes until the tomatoes soften and split.

2 Meanwhile, add the pasta to a large pan of boiling salted water and cook at a fast boil until al dente (tender but firm to the bite).

3 Add the herbs to the sauce, and season with salt and pepper to taste. Drain the pasta and toss with the tomato and chilli sauce. Divide between warm bowls and scatter Parmesan shavings over to serve.

This mouthwatering pasta sauce is typical of southern Italy, where chilli features strongly in many regional dishes.

Pansôti with walnut sauce

Serves 6

For the pasta
250g (9oz) Italian '00' plain flour
½ tsp sea salt
2 medium eggs

For the filling and sauce
60g (2¼oz) chopped chervil
60g (2¼oz) chopped chives
60g (2¼oz) chopped marjoram
2 garlic cloves
1 medium egg

90g (3¼oz) ricotta cheese
125g (4oz) slightly dry, coarse
  breadcrumbs, soaked in water and
  squeezed dry
125g (4oz) shelled walnuts
90g (3¼oz) Parmesan cheese, freshly
  grated
125ml (4fl oz) double cream
4 tbsp extra virgin olive oil
sea salt and pepper

1 To make the pasta, heap the flour in a mound on a board, sprinkle over the salt and make a well in the centre. Break the eggs into the well and gradually work them into the flour, adding sufficient water to make a soft dough. Knead until smooth and elastic. Wrap in cling film and chill for 20 minutes.
2 For the filling, mix the chopped herbs, garlic, egg and ricotta together in a bowl and add half of the soaked breadcrumbs. Mix well, seasoning with salt and pepper to taste.
3 Blanch the walnuts in boiling water for 1 minute, then drain and peel off the skins. Place the nuts in a blender with the remaining soaked breadcrumbs, 1 tbsp Parmesan, the cream and olive oil. Blend to a creamy consistency. Transfer the sauce to a small saucepan and warm gently.
4 Roll out the pasta dough, using a pasta machine, to the second thinnest setting. Cut into 6cm (2½ inch) squares. Place a small amount of filling in the centre of each square and fold the dough back over to form a triangle, pressing the edges together lightly to seal in the filling.
5 Cook the pansôti in plenty of boiling salted water until al dente (tender but firm to the bite), about 3 minutes. Drain and serve topped with the walnut sauce and remaining Parmesan.

Pumpkin ravioli

Illustrated on previous pages

Serves 6

For the pasta

300g (11oz) Italian '00' plain flour

¾ tsp sea salt

3 large eggs

For the stuffing and sage butter

1 small pumpkin, about 1kg (2¼lb)

2 garlic cloves, peeled and crushed

6 amaretti biscuits, finely crumbled

100g (3½oz) Parmesan cheese,
  freshly grated

90g (3¼oz) unsalted butter

handful of sage leaves

sea salt and pepper

1 Preheat the oven to 180°C (fan oven 160°C), gas mark 4. To make the stuffing, cut the pumpkin into large pieces using a sharp knife, and discard the seeds. Place the pumpkin on a foil-lined baking sheet and bake in the oven for 30 minutes. Allow to cool, then remove the skin. Put the pumpkin flesh into a food processor with the garlic and seasoning, and whiz to a purée. Mix the pumpkin purée with the crumbled amaretti and half of the Parmesan. Check the seasoning.

2 To make the pasta, heap the flour into a mound on a board and sprinkle over the salt. Make a well in the centre. Break the eggs into the well and gradually work them into the flour to form a dough. Knead until smooth and elastic.

3 Divide the pasta dough in half and roll out into two very thin sheets of equal size, using a pasta machine if possible. Place small mounds of the pumpkin mixture on one pasta sheet, spacing them about 5cm (2 inches) apart. Top with the second pasta sheet and press lightly around each mound of filling to seal. Cut out the ravioli, using a fluted 5cm (2 inch) round cutter.

4 Bring a large saucepan of salted water to the boil. Drop in the ravioli and cook until al dente (tender but firm to the bite), about 2–3 minutes. Meanwhile, melt the butter in a small saucepan and add the sage leaves.

5 Drain the ravioli and divide between warm plates. Sprinkle with the remaining Parmesan and drizzle with the sage butter. Eat at once.

These small, plump ravioli are filled with pumpkin and crumbled amaretti biscuits, and served drizzled with a fragrant sage butter.

Creamy chicken and mushroom pasta

Serves 4

1 large cooked chicken breast

350g (12oz) dried orecchiette or
  pasta shells

3 tbsp olive oil

125g (4oz) button, oyster or chestnut
  mushrooms, sliced

150ml (¼ pint) dry white wine

4 tbsp single cream

2 tbsp finely chopped rosemary
  leaves

sea salt and pepper

1 Remove the skin from the cooked chicken breast, take the meat off the
bone and cut into bite-sized pieces.

2 Bring a large saucepan of salted water to the boil. Add the pasta and cook
in fast boiling water until al dente (tender but firm to the bite).

3 Heat the olive oil in a sauté pan, add the mushrooms and sauté until
softened. Add the chopped chicken, white wine, cream, chopped rosemary
and salt and pepper. Cook, stirring occasionally, for 5 minutes.

4 Drain the cooked pasta and toss with the sauce. Divide between warm
bowls and serve at once.

Pasta is the ultimate fast food, especially when
it is combined with a speedy sauce. This is an
ideal quick supper if you are too tired and
hungry to spend much time in the kitchen.

Pasta with meatballs in tomato sauce

Illustrated on previous pages

Serves 6

For the meatballs
250g (9oz) lean beef mince
250g (9oz) lean veal mince
125g (4oz) lean pork mince
handful of flat leaf parsley, finely
   chopped
½ tsp oregano leaves, finely chopped
2 tbsp dry vermouth
grated zest of 2 unwaxed lemons
100g (3½oz) soft, white breadcrumbs
2 large eggs
2 garlic cloves, peeled and crushed
sea salt and pepper

For the sauce and pasta
700g jar tomato passata
400g (14oz) dried penne, cellentani
   or macaroni
To serve
Parmesan cheese shavings

1 First, prepare the meatballs. Combine all the ingredients in a bowl and season well with salt and pepper. Mix thoroughly with a wooden spoon until evenly blended. Shape into small balls, about 2cm (¾ inch) in diameter.
2 Pour the passata into a large shallow pan. Bring to a simmer and add the meatballs. Cover and cook over a medium heat for 40 minutes.
3 Towards the end of the cooking time, add the pasta to a large pan of boiling salted water and cook at a fast boil until al dente (tender but firm to the bite). Drain well.
4 Divide the hot pasta between warm bowls and pour the meatballs in tomato sauce over the top. Toss to mix, scatter over Parmesan shavings and serve.

This is a classic dish from Campania, my home region. Minced beef, veal and pork are made into meatballs and cooked in a rich tomato sauce, to be served with pasta. Conveniently, both the sauce and meatballs can be made in advance.

Spaghetti with Italian sausage

Serves 6

350g (12oz) dried spaghetti

sea salt and pepper

For the sauce

750g (1lb 10oz) Italian sausage

2 tbsp olive oil

1 onion, peeled and finely chopped

1 tsp oregano leaves

700g jar tomato passata

1 bay leaf

2 tbsp dry vermouth

To serve

handful of flat leaf parsley, finely
  chopped

1 First prepare the sauce. Cut the sausage into 2.5cm (1 inch) pieces and place in a shallow pan with 6 tbsp water. Bring to a simmer and cook until the water has evaporated.

2 Heat the olive oil in another pan, add the onion and sauté for 5 minutes or until soft, then add the sausage and oregano and cook for a further 5 minutes. Add the tomato passata, bay leaf and vermouth, and simmer uncovered for 30 minutes. Season with salt and pepper to taste.

3 Towards the end of the cooking time, add the spaghetti to a large pan of boiling salted water and cook at a fast boil until al dente (tender but firm to the bite), about 8–10 minutes. Drain well.

4 Divide the spaghetti between warm plates and pour the hot sauce over the top. Sprinkle with parsley and serve straightaway.

This is one of the easiest of the classic pasta dishes to prepare and it's one that is always popular with children.

Chicken lasagne

Serves 6–8

250g pack egg lasagne (no pre-cook)

For the filling

6 chicken breasts

2 tbsp olive oil

2 rosemary sprigs, leaves chopped

1 onion, peeled and finely chopped

175ml (6fl oz) white wine

2 x 400g cans chopped tomatoes

75g (3oz) unsalted butter

2 garlic cloves, peeled and crushed

500g (1lb 2oz) field mushrooms

handful of flat leaf parsley, finely chopped

handful of basil leaves, torn

sea salt and pepper

For the sauce

75g (3oz) unsalted butter

100g (3½oz) Italian '00' flour

600ml (1 pint) milk, warmed

50g (2oz) Parmesan cheese, freshly grated

1 Preheat the oven to 200°C (fan oven 180°C), gas mark 6. For the filling, season the chicken breasts, rub with a little olive oil, place in a roasting tin and sprinkle with the chopped rosemary leaves. Roast for 20 minutes.

2 Meanwhile, heat the remaining olive oil in a saucepan, add the onion and cook for 5 minutes or until softened and golden. Add the wine and let it evaporate. Next add the chopped tomatoes and bring to a simmer. Season with salt and pepper, and simmer for 20 minutes.

3 In the meantime, heat the butter in a frying pan. Add the garlic and mushrooms and sauté until golden, turning once. Season with salt and pepper. Add the mushrooms to the tomatoes, along with the chopped parsley and basil.

4 Cut the cooked chicken breasts into strips and add to the mushroom and tomato mixture. Adjust the seasoning and set aside. Lower the oven setting to 180°C (fan oven 160°C), gas mark 4.

5 To make the sauce, melt the butter in a heavy-based pan, stir in the flour and cook for 1–2 minutes until golden. Add the warmed milk little by little to form a thick sauce, stirring over a medium heat until thick and smooth. Stir in half of the Parmesan and season to taste. (Unless you are assembling the dish straightaway, cover the surface with a damp piece of baking parchment to stop a skin forming.)

6 Line a lasagne dish with a layer of sauce, then cover with a layer of lasagne sheets. Spoon half of the chicken and mushroom mixture on top, then add another layer of lasagne. Cover with the remaining chicken and mushroom mixture, a final layer of lasagne, then the rest of the sauce.

7 Sprinkle with the remaining Parmesan and bake for 25 minutes until golden and bubbling. Serve hot.

Polenta with wild mushrooms

Illustrated on previous pages

Serves 4

For the polenta

200g (7oz) coarse polenta

50g (2oz) unsalted butter, cut into cubes

50g (2oz) Parmesan cheese, freshly grated

sea salt and pepper

For the mushroom sauce

700g (1½lb) wild or cultivated flat mushrooms

4 tbsp olive oil

1 small garlic clove, peeled and crushed

1 tbsp chopped thyme, plus sprigs to serve

150ml (¼ pint) white wine

2 tbsp chopped flat leaf parsley

1 Bring 1.7 litres (3 pints) water to the boil in a large saucepan with 1 tsp salt added. Gradually add the polenta, letting it run through your fingers in a thin stream, and stirring constantly to prevent lumps. Simmer for 35 minutes or until the mixture comes away from the sides of the pan, stirring often.

2 When the polenta is cooked, stir in the butter, Parmesan and pepper to taste. (At this stage, you have what is known as 'wet polenta', which can be served as a simple accompaniment.)

3 While the polenta is still hot, spread it on to a dampened baking sheet or wooden board, to a 1cm (½ inch) thickness. Leave for about 1 hour until softly set.

4 Meanwhile, make the sauce. Halve or quarter any large mushrooms. Heat the olive oil and garlic in a pan, then add the mushrooms and thyme and cook over a high heat for 1 minute. Season with salt and pepper. Add the wine and boil vigorously until almost totally evaporated. Stir in the parsley.

5 Preheat a griddle pan or the grill. Cut the set polenta into triangles and griddle or grill on both sides until lightly charred. Serve on warm plates, topped with the mushroom sauce and a few thyme sprigs.

Here basic polenta is allowed to set, then cut into wedges, griddled and served topped with a wild mushroom sauce. It makes an elegant first course for a special dinner.

Fried polenta sandwiches

Makes 6

For the polenta

600ml (1 pint) vegetable broth
  (page 61) or water
125g (4oz) coarse polenta
25g (1oz) Parmesan cheese, freshly
  grated
25g (1oz) unsalted butter
sea salt and pepper

To assemble and cook

125g (4oz) fontina cheese
6 slices of prosciutto
plain flour, to dust
1 large egg, beaten
175g (6oz) fresh white breadcrumbs
olive oil, for shallow-frying

1 Pour the vegetable broth or water into a large saucepan, add ½ tsp salt and bring to the boil. Gradually add the polenta, letting it run through your fingers in a thin stream, and stirring constantly to prevent lumps forming. Simmer for 30 minutes or until the mixture comes away from the sides of the pan, stirring frequently.

2 When the polenta is cooked, stir in the Parmesan, butter and some pepper. Spread the hot polenta mixture on to a dampened baking sheet or wooden board, to a 1cm (½ inch) thickness. Leave for about 1 hour until set.

3 Cut the polenta into rounds, using a 7.5cm (3 inch) cutter. Cut the fontina into slices, a little smaller than the polenta rounds. Sandwich a slice each of cheese and prosciutto between pairs of polenta rounds. Press well together.

4 Dust the polenta sandwiches with flour to coat all over, then dip into the beaten egg, and finally into the breadcrumbs. Press lightly, so the breadcrumbs adhere.

5 Heat the olive oil in a large frying pan and shallow-fry the polenta sandwiches on both sides until golden brown. Drain on kitchen paper, then serve immediately.

This snack is a delicious way of using up leftover polenta. If you are unable to find fontina, use mozzarella cheese instead.

Rice balls

Serves 4

800ml (1 pint 7fl oz) vegetable broth
(page 61)
50g (2oz) unsalted butter
275g (10oz) risotto rice (such as
vialone nano, carnaroli or arborio)
175g (6oz) mozzarella cheese, cut
into small cubes
6 shallots, peeled and finely chopped
finely grated zest of 1 large
unwaxed orange

handful of mixed herbs (such as flat
leaf parsley, basil and oregano),
chopped
6 tbsp freshly grated Parmesan
cheese
sea salt and pepper
To assemble and cook
1 egg, lightly beaten
50g (2oz) fresh white breadcrumbs
6 tbsp olive oil

1 Heat the broth in a saucepan until almost boiling, then reduce the heat and
keep at a low simmer.
2 Heat the butter in a wide, heavy-based saucepan. Add the rice and stir,
using a wooden spoon, until the grains are well coated and glistening, about
1 minute. Add a ladleful of hot broth and simmer, stirring, until it has been
absorbed. Continue to add the broth at intervals and cook as before, until all
the liquid has been absorbed and the rice is al dente (tender but retaining a
bite), about 18–20 minutes.
3 Add the mozzarella, shallots, orange zest, mixed herbs, Parmesan and salt
and pepper to taste. Mix well. Remove from the heat and allow to cool. (The
rice is easier to handle and shape when it is cold.)
4 Using your hands, shape the rice mixture into 8 balls. Dip each one into
the beaten egg and coat well, then roll in the breadcrumbs to coat. Use your
fingers to press crumbs on to any uncoated surface.
5 Heat the olive oil in a frying pan. Fry the rice balls, in batches if necessary,
turning until golden on all sides, about 8 minutes. Drain well on kitchen
paper. Serve hot or cold.

Enjoyed throughout Italy, these cheesy rice
balls can be made with leftover risotto.

Saffron risotto

Serves 4

900ml (1½ pints) vegetable broth
  (page 61)
50g (2oz) unsalted butter
1 tbsp olive oil
8 shallots, peeled and finely chopped
½ tsp saffron threads
275g (10oz) risotto rice (such as
  vialone nano, carnaroli or arborio)

about 75ml (2½fl oz) white wine
100g (3½oz) Parmesan cheese,
  freshly grated, plus extra to serve
2 tbsp single cream
handful of flat leaf parsley, coarsely
  chopped (optional)
sea salt and pepper

1 Heat the broth in a saucepan until almost boiling, then reduce the heat and keep at a low simmer.

2 Heat the butter and olive oil in a wide, heavy-based saucepan over a medium heat. Add the shallots and cook for 1–2 minutes, until softened but not browned. Add the saffron and stir until its yellow colour is released, then add the rice. Stir with a wooden spoon until the rice grains are well coated and glistening, about 1 minute.

3 Add the wine and stir until absorbed. Add a ladleful of hot broth and simmer, stirring until it has been absorbed. Continue to add the broth at intervals and cook as before, until the liquid is absorbed and the rice is al dente (tender but retaining a bite), about 18–20 minutes. Save the last ladleful of broth.

4 Add the Parmesan, cream, reserved broth, chopped parsley if using, and some salt and pepper. Stir well, then remove from the heat, cover and leave to rest for 2 minutes. Spoon into warm bowls and serve with extra Parmesan.

This classic 'risotto alla milanese' is a famous speciality of Lombardy. I use saffron threads rather than the powdered form, which tends to be of a lesser quality and flavour.

Tomato risotto

Serves 4

900ml (1½ pints) vegetable broth (page 61)
50g (2oz) unsalted butter
1 tbsp olive oil
8 shallots, peeled and finely chopped
2 garlic cloves, peeled and crushed
275g (10oz) risotto rice (such as vialone nano, carnaroli or arborio)
about 75ml (2½fl oz) white wine

8 firm, ripe tomatoes, deseeded and coarsely chopped
100g (3½oz) Parmesan cheese, freshly grated
large handful of basil leaves, torn
sea salt and pepper

To serve (optional)
freshly grated Parmesan cheese
handful of basil leaves, torn

1 Put the vegetable broth into a saucepan. Heat until almost boiling, then reduce the heat until barely simmering to keep it hot.

2 Heat the butter and olive oil in a wide, heavy-based saucepan over a medium heat. Add the shallots and cook for 1–2 minutes until softened but not browned. Add the garlic and mix well.

3 Add the rice and stir, using a wooden spoon, until the grains are well coated and glistening, about 1 minute. Pour in the wine and stir until it has been completely absorbed.

4 Add a ladleful of hot broth and simmer, stirring, until it has been absorbed. Continue to add the broth in this way then, after 10 minutes, add the tomatoes. Add the rest of the broth at intervals and cook as before, for a further 8–10 minutes, until the liquid has been absorbed and the rice is al dente (tender but retaining a bite). Reserve the last ladleful of broth.

5 Stir in the Parmesan, reserved broth, basil, salt and pepper. Remove from the heat, cover and leave to rest for 2 minutes. Spoon into warm bowls, sprinkle with grated Parmesan and basil if using, and serve.

The simplicity of this dish appeals to me and probably accounts for its popularity with children as well as grown-ups.

Risotto with asparagus, peas and basil

Serves 4
900ml (1½ pints) vegetable broth
  (page 61)
50g (2oz) unsalted butter
1 tbsp olive oil
8 shallots, peeled and finely chopped
275g (10oz) risotto rice (such as
  vialone nano, carnaroli or arborio)
about 75ml (2½fl oz) white wine
150g (5oz) podded fresh or frozen
  peas (thawed)

350g (12oz) asparagus spears, cut
  into 4cm (1½ inch) lengths
finely grated zest of 1 unwaxed lemon
100g (3½oz) Parmesan cheese,
  freshly grated
large handful of basil leaves, torn
sea salt and pepper
To serve (optional)
handful of basil leaves, torn
freshly grated Parmesan cheese

1 Put the vegetable broth into a saucepan. Heat until almost boiling, then reduce the heat until barely simmering to keep it hot.
2 Heat the butter and olive oil in a wide, heavy-based saucepan over a medium heat. Add the shallots and cook for 1–2 minutes until softened but not browned.
3 Add the rice and stir, using a wooden spoon, until the grains are well coated and glistening, about 1 minute. Pour in the wine and stir until it has been completely absorbed.
4 Add a ladleful of hot broth and simmer, stirring, until it has been absorbed. Continue to add the broth in this way then, after 10 minutes, add the fresh peas if using, asparagus and lemon zest and mix well. Continue to add the broth at intervals and cook as before, for a further 8–10 minutes, until the liquid has been absorbed and the rice is al dente (tender but retaining a bite). If using frozen peas, add 2 minutes before the end of cooking. Reserve the last ladleful of broth.
5 Add the Parmesan, reserved broth, basil, salt and pepper. Mix well. Remove from the heat, cover and leave to rest for 2 minutes. Spoon into warm bowls and top with more basil and grated Parmesan if using. Serve immediately.

easy
fish and
shellfish

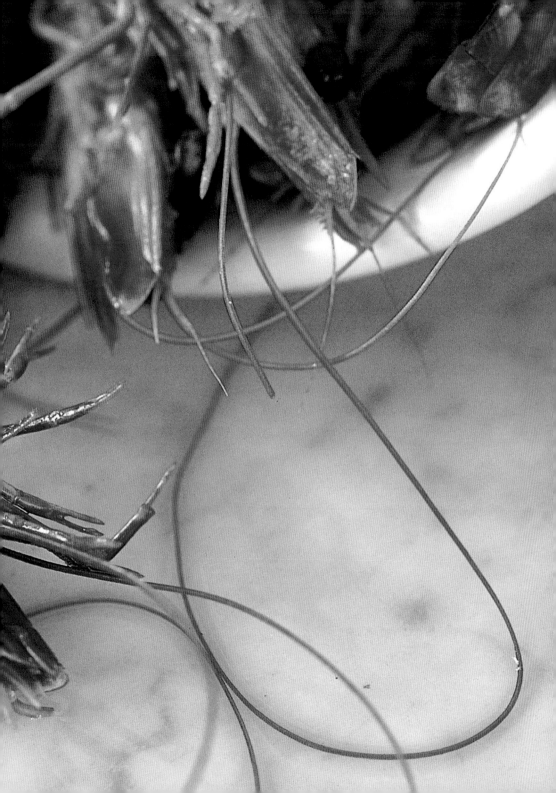

Prawns and white beans Venetian style

Serves 4

125g (4oz) dried cannellini beans, soaked in cold water overnight

2 rosemary sprigs

3 bay leaves

3 thyme sprigs

3 flat leaf parsley sprigs

4 garlic cloves, unpeeled

500g (1lb 2oz) large raw prawns in shell

2 celery stalks, finely chopped

juice of 1 lemon

handful of flat leaf parsley, chopped

2–3 tbsp extra virgin olive oil

sea salt and pepper

lemon wedges, to serve

1 Drain the cannellini beans and place in a large pan. Add plenty of cold water to cover, and the herbs and unpeeled garlic. Bring to the boil, then reduce the heat and cook for about 1½ pints hours or until the beans are tender. Drain the beans and discard the herbs and garlic.

2 Add the prawns to a pan of boiling salted water and simmer for 2 minutes or until they just turn pink. Immediately drain, peel and devein them.

3 Combine the beans and prawns in a bowl and add the celery, along with the lemon juice and parsley. Season well with salt and pepper, drizzle with the extra virgin olive oil and toss to mix. Serve with lemon wedges.

Venetians love seafood, and the combination of prawns and beans in this delicate salad is delicious, and the textures are diverse.

Fritto misto

Illustrated on previous pages

Serves 6

300g (11oz) squid

300g (11oz) scampi tails or large
  raw prawns in shell

300g (11oz) monkfish fillet, skinned

125g (4oz) Italian '00' flour, to coat

oil, for deep-frying

sea salt

lemon wedges, to serve

1 To clean whole squid, pull the pouch and tentacles apart and remove the
transparent quill from the pouch. Cut the tentacles away from the head just
below the eyes and discard the head, reserving the tentacles. Peel off the
transparent outer skin covering the pouch, then cut into rings. Baby squid
can simply be halved.

2 Peel away the shell from the prawns, leaving the tail end intact if you like.
Prise out the dark intestinal vein that runs down the back.

3 Cut the monkfish into cubes. Wash all the seafood and dry it well on
kitchen paper. Scatter the flour on a board or tray and toss the seafood in it
to coat each piece thoroughly.

4 Heat the oil in a deep-fat fryer or deep heavy-based saucepan to 190°C, or
until a cube of bread dropped in browns in 30 seconds. Deep-fry the seafood,
a few pieces at a time, until golden and cooked through, about 2–3 minutes.

5 Drain on kitchen paper, sprinkle with salt and serve at once accompanied
by lemon wedges.

This dish of mixed fried fish is very popular throughout Italy. In my native Campania, it is usually made of tiny squid, cuttlefish rings and scampi.

Stuffed sardines

Serves 4
800g (1¾lb) fresh sardines, cleaned
5 tbsp white breadcrumbs (slightly
  dry)
1 tbsp chopped rosemary leaves,
  plus an extra stem

2 tbsp chopped flat leaf parsley
2 garlic cloves, peeled and finely
  chopped
6 tbsp olive oil
juice of 2 lemons
sea salt and pepper

1 Preheat the oven to 200°C (fan oven 180°C), gas mark 6. Cut off the heads from the sardines. Slit down the underside, open out the fish and place flesh-side down on a board. Press down along the spine to flatten and loosen the backbone, then turn over and remove the bone. Wash the fish and pat dry.
2 For the stuffing, put the breadcrumbs, rosemary, parsley, garlic and some seasoning into a bowl. Pour in 4 tbsp of the olive oil and mix thoroughly.
3 With the open sardines skin-side down, divide the stuffing between them, spreading it along the middle of each fish. Fold the sides together, so the sardines resume their original shape.
4 Place the sardines, side by side, in a lightly oiled roasting tray in which they fit snugly in a single layer. Sprinkle with salt and pepper. Drizzle with the remaining olive oil and the lemon juice, and lay the rosemary stem on top (for extra flavour). Bake for about 15 minutes until the fish are cooked and a little crispy on top. Serve warm.

Sardines are stuffed in many different ways all around the Italian coast. The rosemary and garlic in this dish identify it as Venetian.

Red mullet in an envelope

Illustrated on previous pages

Serves 4

4 red mullet, each about 200g (7oz),
   cleaned
4 fennel frond sprigs
large handful of basil leaves
large handful of rosemary leaves
2 tbsp olive oil
sea salt and pepper

For the anchovy butter

125g (4oz) unsalted butter, softened
6–8 anchovy fillets in oil, drained

1 Preheat the oven to 220°C (fan oven 200°C), gas mark 7. For the anchovy butter, put the softened butter into a bowl, add the anchovy fillets and mash together, using a fork. Chill until ready to use.

2 Rinse and dry the fish well, and put some of the herbs into each cavity. Cut 4 large rectangles of baking parchment (large enough to envelop the fish). Brush the red mullet with olive oil, then place a fish in the centre of each parchment rectangle.

3 Sprinkle more herbs on top of the fish and season with salt and pepper. Bring the long edges of the paper up over the fish and fold together firmly. Twist the ends of the paper to seal. Place the parcels on a baking tray and bake in the oven for 15–20 minutes.

4 Serve the fish in their fragrant parcels, to be opened at the table.

Baking red mullet in sealed paper parcels is an excellent way of retaining their delicate flavour and enticing aroma as they cook. Ask your fishmonger to clean the fish, leaving the liver in if possible, as this adds to the flavour.

Swordfish steaks with capers and anchovies

Serves 4

4 swordfish steaks, each about
225g (8oz)
6 tbsp olive oil, plus extra to oil
3 tbsp dry white wine
juice of 1 lemon

2 shallots, peeled and finely chopped
1 tbsp small capers, rinsed
4 anchovy fillets in oil, drained and
chopped
sea salt and pepper

1 Place the swordfish steaks in a shallow dish in a single layer. Mix the olive oil with the white wine and lemon juice, and pour over the swordfish steaks. Scatter over the shallots, capers and anchovies. Cover and leave to marinate in a cool place for 1 hour.

2 Heat a ridged cast-iron griddle pan, or preheat the grill to high and brush the griddle (or grill) pan with olive oil. Lift the fish steaks from the dish, reserving the marinade, and place on the griddle or grill pan.

3 Cook the fish steaks for about 6 minutes on each side depending on thickness, basting frequently with the reserved marinade. Season with salt and pepper to taste and serve, with a mixed salad.

Fish steaks benefit from being marinated before cooking, especially if they are to be griddled, grilled or barbecued. An oil-based marinade helps to prevent them becoming dry.

Monkfish spiedini

Serves 4

1kg (2¼lb) monkfish tail, filleted and
skinned
juice of 2 lemons
2 garlic cloves, peeled and finely
chopped

1 red chilli, deseeded and chopped
1–2 tsp finely chopped rosemary
leaves
4 tbsp olive oil
sea salt and pepper

1 Cut the monkfish fillet into 2.5cm (1 inch) cubes and place in a shallow
dish. Mix the lemon juice with the chopped garlic, chilli, chopped rosemary
and olive oil. Pour over the fish and leave to marinate in a cool place for
about 1 hour.

2 Preheat the grill. Thread the monkfish on to 4 or 8 skewers. Grill for
about 1½ minutes on each of the 4 sides, basting occasionally with the
marinade. Season with salt and pepper. Serve at once.

Firm-textured monkfish is ideal for grilling or
barbecueing. Marinating it first in an oil-based
marinade helps to keep the fish moist and
succulent under the grill.

Trout with parsley and lemon cream sauce

Serves 4

4 trout, each about 225g (8oz),
  cleaned
1.2 litres (2 pints) fish broth (page 65)
  or vegetable broth (page 61)
sea salt and pepper

For the sauce

50g (2oz) unsalted butter
250ml (8fl oz) double cream
juice of 2 lemons

To serve

handful of flat leaf parsley, finely
  chopped

1 Rinse the trout inside and out. Bring the fish or vegetable broth to the boil in a wide, shallow pan. Place the trout in the broth and poach gently just until the flesh is opaque and the eyes are white, about 10 minutes. Lift out and drain well.

2 Meanwhile, make the sauce. Melt the butter in a small saucepan, then add the cream, lemon juice and some salt. Bring to a simmer, stirring constantly, and simmer for about 5 minutes until reduced and slightly thickened. Taste and adjust the seasoning.

3 Place the trout on warm plates. Pour the sauce over the fish, then scatter generously with chopped parsley and serve at once.

Freshwater trout are abundant in the rivers of the mountainous Trentino area in the north of Italy, which borders Austria. Here they are served with a lemon and parsley cream sauce.

Sea bass fillets with lemon and chilli

Serves 4

4 sea bass fillets, each about
200g (7oz)
finely grated zest and juice of
2 lemons
4 tbsp olive oil

1 red chilli, deseeded and finely
chopped
1 garlic clove, peeled and finely
chopped
1 red onion, peeled and finely sliced
sea salt and pepper

1 Place the sea bass fillets, skin-side down, in a shallow ovenproof dish. In a bowl, combine the lemon zest and juice, olive oil, chilli, garlic and red onion. Pour the mixture over the fish, cover and leave to marinate in a cool place for about 1 hour.

2 Preheat the oven to 200°C (fan oven 180°C), gas mark 6. Season the fish with salt and pepper and bake in the oven for 12–15 minutes or until just tender. Serve at once.

Fish is very popular throughout Italy. Not surprisingly, it is especially important along the extensive Italian coastline.

Whole fish baked in tomato sauce

Serves 4

1 sea bream, about 1.4kg (3lb), or
   other whole white fish, cleaned
   and boned out
1–2 tbsp olive oil
sea salt and pepper

For the sauce

4 tbsp olive oil
1 onion, peeled and finely chopped
1 small celery stalk, finely chopped
1 garlic clove, peeled and finely
   chopped
1 tbsp chopped flat leaf parsley
8 tomatoes, skinned and coarsely
   chopped
150ml (¼ pint) dry white wine

1 Preheat the oven to 200°C (fan oven 180°C), gas mark 6. Wash and pat the fish dry, then season with salt inside and out. Place in an oiled roasting tin and brush the skin with olive oil.

2 For the sauce, heat the olive oil in a pan, add the onion, celery, garlic and parsley, and sauté until the vegetables are soft. Add the tomatoes and wine and cook for 10 minutes. Season with salt and pepper to taste.

3 Spoon the sauce over and around the fish. Cover the tin with foil and bake in the oven for about 30 minutes until the fish is cooked. To test, insert a knife into the thickest part of the body and lift out a little of the flesh – it should be opaque but still moist.

4 Carefully transfer the fish to a warm serving platter and spoon the sauce around. Serve at once.

Baking a whole fish in a sauce is a good way of keeping the fish succulent, while imparting extra flavour at the same time. Try other white fish, such as sea bass, hake or haddock.

Stuffed sole in saffron sauce

Serves 6

3 Dover soles, filleted
2 tbsp sultanas
125g (4oz) young, tender spinach
   leaves, stalks removed
2 tbsp pine nuts
2 shallots, peeled and very finely
   chopped

600ml (1 pint) fish broth (page 65)
20 saffron threads
125ml (4fl oz) dry white wine
40g (1½oz) unsalted butter, cut into
   small pieces
sea salt and pepper

1 Rinse the sole fillets and pat dry. Put the sultanas into a bowl, add
3–4 tbsp hot water and leave for 10 minutes to plump up. Drain and pat dry
with kitchen paper.
2 Season the sole fillets with salt and pepper on both sides. Lay the spinach
leaves overlapping on each fillet and place some sultanas, pine nuts and
chopped shallot on top. Roll up the fillets and secure them with string or
wooden cocktail sticks.
3 Bring the fish broth to the boil in a wide, shallow pan. Turn the heat
down, then add the fish bundles and cover the pan. Poach gently, with the
liquid barely simmering, for 6 minutes.
4 Meanwhile put the saffron threads into a small mortar and pound with the
pestle until crushed. Add a spoonful or two of the hot fish liquid to dissolve
the mixture.
5 Using a slotted spoon, remove the sole bundles from the fish broth and
place on a warm plate; keep hot. Pour off half of the broth. Add the saffron
mixture and wine to the remaining broth in the pan and boil to reduce by
half over a high heat. Stir in the pieces of butter, a few at a time.
6 When all the butter has been incorporated, taste and adjust the seasoning.
Spoon the sauce around the sole bundles and serve.

Roasted monkfish with garlic

Illustrated on previous pages

Serves 4

1kg (2¼lb) monkfish tail, filleted and skinned

1 large garlic bulb, as fresh as possible

4–5 bay leaves

50ml (2fl oz) olive oil

1 tsp thyme leaves

½ tsp fennel seeds (optional)

juice of 1 lemon

sea salt and pepper

1 Preheat the oven to 200°C (fan oven 180°C), gas mark 6. Remove all traces of the thin, grey membrane covering the monkfish, then rinse and dry the fish. To hold the fillets together, tie a length of string around the length of the fish, then secure with string at intervals (as shown).

2 Peel 2 garlic cloves from the bulb and cut them into thin slices. Make some incisions in the fish and push in the garlic slices. Tuck the bay leaves under the string.

3 Preheat a baking tray in the oven for a few minutes. Add half of the olive oil, then lay the fish on the hot tray and turn carefully to coat with the hot oil. Season with salt and pepper, and scatter with the thyme leaves and fennel seeds if using. Drizzle the lemon juice and remaining olive oil over the fish and surround with the rest of the unpeeled garlic cloves.

4 Roast in the oven for 20–30 minutes, basting frequently. Serve with grilled tomatoes if you like.

Monkfish has a meaty texture and its flavour is exquisite. Ask your fishmonger to skin and fillet the monkfish by removing the central bone to give two meaty fillets.

Tuna steaks with capers

Serves 4

4 tuna or swordfish steaks, each
    about 225g (8oz)
250ml (8fl oz) dry white wine
1 rosemary sprig, finely chopped
4 garlic cloves, peeled and finely
    chopped
olive oil, to brush
2 tbsp day-old white breadcrumbs,
    lightly toasted
sea salt and pepper

For the dressing:

4 tbsp extra virgin olive oil
finely grated zest and juice of
    1 unwaxed lemon
1 tbsp salted capers, soaked in cold
    water for 20 minutes and drained

1 Place the fish steaks in a shallow dish and season with salt and pepper.
Add the wine, rosemary and garlic, and turn the steaks to coat all over.
Leave to marinate for at least an hour.
2 Drain the fish and pat dry, reserving the marinade. Heat a ridged cast-iron
griddle pan, or preheat the grill to high and brush the griddle (or grill) pan
with olive oil. Cook the fish steaks for about 6–8 minutes on each side
depending on thickness, basting frequently with the reserved marinade.
3 Meanwhile, make the dressing. In a small bowl, whisk the olive oil with
the lemon juice and zest, capers, and some salt and pepper.
4 Sprinkle the cooked tuna or swordfish with the toasted breadcrumbs. Place
on warm plates and drizzle with the dressing. Serve with a mixed leaf salad.

Fine quality swordfish and tuna are caught
off the Sicilian coast and this dish is a
speciality of the island. The grilled fish steaks
are served with a sauce of capers and lemon –
both found in abundance on Sicily.

Tuna and spinach pie

Serves 4

300g (11oz) medium old potatoes (Desirée, Pentland Crown, King Edward)

5 tbsp olive oil, plus extra to brush

fine dried breadcrumbs, to coat tin

1kg (2¼lb) spinach, tough stalks removed

1 onion, peeled and finely chopped

1 garlic clove, peeled and very finely chopped

handful of flat leaf parsley, chopped

generous grating of nutmeg

2 eggs, plus 1 egg yolk

6 tbsp freshly grated Parmesan cheese

125g (4oz) canned tuna or bottled tuna in best quality olive oil

2 anchovy fillets in oil, drained and chopped

sea salt and pepper

1 Cook the potatoes in their skins in boiling salted water until soft, about 20 minutes. Drain and peel. Mash the potatoes smoothly, using a potato ricer, or food processor fitted with a fine grating disc, or by hand. Add 2 tbsp of the olive oil to the potato purée and mix well.

2 Preheat the oven to 190°C (fan oven 170°C), gas mark 5. Line an 18cm (7 inch) spring-release cake tin with greaseproof paper or baking parchment, then brush with a little olive oil. Sprinkle the base and sides with breadcrumbs to coat, then carefully shake out any excess.

3 Wash the spinach well and place in a large pan with only the water that clings to the leaves after washing and 1 tsp salt. Cook over a medium high heat until wilted and tender. Drain thoroughly and, as soon as it is cool enough to handle, squeeze out as much moisture as possible using your hands. Chop the spinach coarsely.

4 Heat 3 tbsp olive oil in a sauté pan, add the onion and cook gently for about 5 minutes. Now add the garlic and parsley, then mix in the spinach and nutmeg, turning it over frequently. Add the contents of the pan to the potato purée.

5 Add the eggs, egg yolk, Parmesan and some pepper, then flake the tuna into the mixture and add the anchovy fillets. Mix well, then taste and adjust the seasoning.

6 Spoon the tuna and potato mixture into the prepared tin and bake in the oven for 40 minutes. Serve warm or at room temperature.

Stuffed braised squid

Serves 4–6

12 medium squid, 10–12cm
  (4–5 inches) long, cleaned and
  tentacles reserved (see page 174)
3 tbsp olive oil, plus extra to oil dish
1 onion, peeled and sliced
1 garlic clove, unpeeled
2 large plum tomatoes, skinned,
  deseeded and coarsely chopped
1 tbsp chopped flat leaf parsley
450g (1lb) old potatoes (King Edward,
  Desirée, Pentland Crown)
1 small hot red chilli, deseeded and
  chopped
40g (1½oz) pecorino cheese, grated
sea salt and pepper

For the stuffing

150g (5oz) dry, firm-textured bread,
  torn into small pieces
1 medium egg, lightly beaten
1 garlic clove, peeled and finely
  chopped
1 tbsp chopped flat leaf parsley
finely grated zest of 1 unwaxed
  lemon

To serve

flat leaf parsley leaves

1 First make the stuffing. Put the bread into a small bowl, add just enough warm water to cover and leave to soak for 5 minutes. Drain and squeeze dry. Mix the bread with the rest of the stuffing ingredients, and season with salt and pepper.

2 Spoon the stuffing into the squid pouches, only half filling them to allow room for expansion during cooking. Seal the open end of the squid pouches with wooden cocktail sticks.

3 Preheat the oven to 180°C (fan oven 160°C), gas mark 4 (unless you prefer to cook the dish on the hob). Lightly oil a 3 litre (5 pint) round casserole (flameproof if cooking on the hob). Scatter the onion, garlic, tomatoes, parsley and 3 tbsp water in the dish and season with salt and pepper.

4 Peel the potatoes and cut into 1cm (½ inch) thick slices. Arrange slightly overlapping on top of the onion and tomato mixture and sprinkle with the chilli and more salt and pepper. Arrange the stuffed squid pouches and tentacles on top. Sprinkle with the cheese and drizzle with 3 tbsp olive oil.

5 Cover and cook in the oven for about 45 minutes, or simmer slowly over a low heat on the hob for 1 hour until the squid and potatoes are tender. Check the casserole occasionally to be sure it remains at a slow simmer. Scatter with parsley and serve.

easy
poultry
and meat

Chicken breasts with a vegetable relish

Serves 4

4 chicken breast fillets (with skin),
  each about 150g (5oz)
1 tbsp chopped sage
2 tbsp olive oil
900g (2lb) onions, peeled and very
  finely sliced
sea salt and pepper

For the vegetable relish

1 yellow pepper, about 150g (5oz)
125g (4oz) aubergine
100g (3½oz) celery
200ml (7fl oz) red wine vinegar
4 tbsp olive oil
1 tbsp tomato purée
1 tbsp caster sugar

1 Preheat the oven to 200°C (fan oven 180°C), gas mark 6. Rub the chicken breasts all over with salt, pepper and chopped sage. Use half of the olive oil to oil a small roasting tin or shallow baking dish.

2 For the relish, cut the vegetables into small pieces, each about 1cm (½ inch). Put them into a saucepan with the wine vinegar and pour in 200ml (7fl oz) water; the liquid should be level with the vegetables. Add 1 tsp salt. Bring to the boil, lower the heat and simmer for 10 minutes.

3 Meanwhile, lay the seasoned chicken breasts in the dish and scatter the onions on top. Sprinkle with salt and pepper and pour over the remaining olive oil. Bake for 20 minutes or until the chicken is tender and cooked through. To test, pierce the thickest part with the tip of a knife; the juices should run clear (not at all pink). The onion should be just tender, crisp on the top and juicy underneath.

4 In the meantime, drain the relish vegetables. Heat the olive oil in a frying pan and stir in the tomato purée and sugar. Cook for about 2 minutes, to caramelise the sugar. Now add the vegetables and turn to coat them in the caramelised sugar and oil mixture. Turn the heat down and cook for a further 15 minutes, stirring frequently. The vegetables should be just crisp. Season with salt and pepper.

5 Spoon the vegetable relish on to warm plates and top with the baked chicken breasts to serve.

Pancetta-wrapped stuffed chicken breasts

Serves 4

4 chicken breast fillets with
skin, preferably corn-fed, each
150g (5oz)
handful of baby spinach leaves

4 tbsp cream cheese
100g (3½oz) button mushrooms,
sliced
8 slices of pancetta
sea salt and pepper

1 Preheat the oven to 200°C (fan oven 180°C), gas mark 6. Cut a deep pocket
horizontally in each chicken breast. Fill each pocket with a few baby spinach
leaves, 1 tbsp cream cheese and 2–3 sliced mushrooms.
2 Season the chicken breasts well, then wrap each chicken breast in 2 slices
of pancetta. Place in a baking dish and bake for 20–25 minutes or until the
pancetta is crisp and the chicken is cooked through.
3 Serve at once, with a green salad.

Chicken breasts are stuffed with a creamy
spinach and mushroom filling, then wrapped
in slices of pancetta to impart flavour and
keep them moist during baking.

Braised lemon chicken

Illustrated on previous pages

Serves 4

1 free-range chicken, about 1.5kg
  (3¼lb), cut into 8 pieces
2–3 tbsp plain flour, to dust
3 tbsp olive oil
thinly pared zest of 3 lemons, finely
  chopped
1 small onion, peeled and finely
  chopped
2 sage sprigs, leaves only, chopped
350ml (12fl oz) dry white wine
sea salt and pepper

1 Pat the chicken pieces dry with kitchen paper, then dust with flour to coat lightly all over.

2 Heat the olive oil in a large, heavy-based sauté pan over a medium high heat. Add the chicken pieces to the pan, and brown well on all sides. Using a slotted spoon, transfer the chicken to a plate and season with salt and pepper to taste.

3 Reduce the heat to medium low and add the lemon zest, onion and sage to the oil remaining in the pan. Sauté until the onion is golden and tender, about 10 minutes.

4 Return the chicken pieces to the pan, along with the juices that have accumulated on the plate. Pour the wine over the chicken, partially cover the pan and simmer gently for 50–55 minutes or until the chicken is very tender and most of the wine has evaporated. The chicken should be nutty brown in colour and glazed with the pan juices. Check the seasoning.

5 Arrange the chicken pieces on warm plates. Skim the fat from the pan juices, taste and adjust the seasoning. If too thick, stir in 1–2 tbsp water. Pour the juices over the chicken and serve.

A light, lemony chicken casserole, best served with some crusty bread to mop up the juices, and perhaps a leafy salad. You could use chicken pieces – meaty thighs would be ideal.

Chicken with tomato and rosemary sauce

Illustrated on previous pages

Serves 4–6

1 free-range chicken, about 1.5kg
(3¼lb), cut into about 8 pieces
1 unwaxed lemon, halved
2 tbsp olive oil
50g (2oz) unsalted butter
150ml (¼ pint) dry white wine
1 onion, peeled and finely chopped
1 garlic clove, peeled and finely
chopped
sea salt and pepper

For the sauce

3 shallots or 1 small onion, peeled
leaves from 2–3 rosemary sprigs
coarsely grated zest of 1 unwaxed
lemon
½ dried red chilli
3 tbsp olive oil
400g (14oz) can chopped tomatoes

To serve

few small rosemary sprigs

1 Wash the chicken pieces and pat dry with kitchen paper. Rub them with
the lemon halves, squeezing out the juice as you do so.

2 Heat the olive oil and butter in a large sauté pan. When the butter begins
to foam, add the chicken pieces and fry on all sides until golden brown. Add
the white wine, bring to the boil and let bubble for 1 minute. Turn the heat
down and add the onion. Cook for a few minutes to soften, then add the
garlic and some salt and pepper. Cook for 20 minutes, turning the chicken
from time to time.

3 While the chicken is cooking, prepare the sauce. Chop the shallots or
onion, rosemary leaves, lemon zest and chilli very finely together. Heat the
olive oil in a frying pan and, when hot, add the finely chopped ingredients.
Sauté very gently for 5 minutes or so, then add the chopped tomatoes and
some salt. Cook for 15 minutes, stirring frequently.

4 Now that the sauce is cooked, add it to the chicken, and stir to mix in the
cooking juices at the bottom of the sauté pan. Leave over a gentle heat for
another 15 minutes, to allow the chicken to absorb the flavours of the sauce.
Taste and adjust the seasoning, then serve scattered with rosemary.

Pancetta and vegetable spiedini

Illustrated on previous pages

Serves 4

250g (9oz) piece of pancetta
8 large field mushrooms, wiped
1 large red onion, peeled

1 large courgette, trimmed
4 sage leaves
olive oil, to baste
sea salt and pepper

1 Preheat the grill. Cut the pancetta into fork-friendly pieces. Quarter the field mushrooms, cut the red onion into wedges, and cut the courgette into chunky rounds.

2 Thread the pancetta, mushroom quarters, onion wedges and courgette chunks on to 4 skewers, adding a sage leaf to each skewer.

3 Cook under the preheated grill, turning occasionally and basting frequently with olive oil, until the vegetables and pancetta are cooked, about 10–15 minutes. Season with salt and pepper. Serve with warm bread.

Of the many Italian cured meats, pancetta is probably the most useful in cooking. Here it enriches, moisturises and adds a wonderful flavour to grilled vegetables.

Pheasant with olives

Serves 2

1 oven-ready pheasant
50g (2oz) pancetta or rindless
   streaky bacon, sliced
125g (4oz) pitted black olives
1 tbsp fennel seeds

15g (½oz) unsalted butter
2 tbsp olive oil
1 tbsp juniper berries, crushed
125ml (4fl oz) dry white wine
50ml (2fl oz) chicken broth (page 64)
sea salt and pepper

1 Preheat the oven to 190°C (fan oven 170°C), gas mark 5. Put the pheasant on a board, wrap the pancetta or bacon slices around the breasts and tie securely. This helps to keep the breast meat moist during roasting. Put the olives and fennel seeds into the pheasant cavity and secure with string.

2 Heat the butter and olive oil in a flameproof casserole over a medium heat and brown the pheasant slowly, turning frequently, for 20 minutes. Season with salt and pepper, and add the juniper berries. Pour in the wine and let it bubble to evaporate.

3 Add the chicken broth and place the casserole in the oven. Roast for about 30 minutes, basting frequently with the pan juices.

4 Cut the pheasant into serving pieces and arrange on a platter with the olives and fennel seeds. Place the casserole over a medium heat, add a little water or extra wine to deglaze and scrape up the browned bits from the bottom, using a wooden spoon. Pour this sauce through a sieve over the pheasant and serve, with a salad or vegetables of your choice.

In Italy, pheasant is hung for 2 or 3 days – half the time typical in this country. Here I have roasted the bird simply with olives, juniper berries, fennel seeds and pancetta.

Osso bucco con gremolata

Illustrated on previous pages

Serves 6

6 pieces of veal shank (osso bucco),
  cut about 4cm (1½ inches) thick
2–3 tbsp plain flour, to dust
25g (1oz) unsalted butter
125ml (4fl oz) dry white wine
finely pared zest and juice of
  2 lemons
handful of flat leaf parsley, finely
  chopped
1 anchovy fillet in oil, drained and
  chopped
sea salt and pepper

1 Dredge the veal pieces in the flour, shaking off the excess. Melt the butter in a large, deep frying pan or sauté pan, then arrange the veal pieces in it. Brown over a medium heat, then turn carefully and brown the other side.
2 Pour in the wine and allow it to evaporate almost completely. Add some salt and pepper, cover tightly and cook very gently for about 1½ hours, adding a little water from time to time to ensure there is some liquid in the bottom of the pan.
3 Chop the lemon zest and mix with the parsley; set aside. Add the anchovy and lemon juice to the stew. Sprinkle the lemon and parsley mix over the top and serve immediately.

This famous dish of braised veal shanks originates from Lombardy. Here they are served topped with my tangy version of the traditional gremolata accompaniment.

Beef braised in Barolo

Serves 6

1kg (2¼lb) joint of braising beef
  (topside or top rump)
2 carrots, peeled and chopped
1 medium onion, peeled and roughly
  chopped
2 celery stalks, roughly chopped
handful of flat leaf parsley

3 bay leaves
1 tbsp juniper berries
1 tsp black peppercorns
350ml (12fl oz) aged Barolo wine, or
  other full-bodied red wine
15g (½oz) unsalted butter, in pieces
1 tbsp olive oil
sea salt and pepper

1 Put the meat into a bowl and add the chopped vegetables, herbs, juniper berries and peppercorns. Pour the wine over the meat, cover the bowl and marinate in the fridge for at least 24 hours.

2 Preheat the oven to 180°C (fan oven 160°C), gas mark 4. Remove the meat from the bowl and dry well, reserving the marinade. Make little slits in the surface of the meat and insert the pieces of butter. Strain the marinade, saving the vegetables and flavourings, as well as the liquor.

3 Heat the olive oil in a flameproof casserole. Add the meat and brown over a medium high heat on all sides.

4 Add the reserved vegetables and flavourings to the meat. Pour in 250ml (8fl oz) of the reserved liquor and some salt. Cover and braise in the oven for about 3 hours, adding more of the reserved wine as needed to keep the meat from drying out.

5 When the meat is cooked, lift out and place on a warm platter; keep warm. Discard the bay leaves. Put the vegetables and other flavourings through a food mill with the cooking liquor (or whiz in a food processor). Reheat this sauce, check the seasoning and pour over the meat to serve.

This is a fine, robust dish from the region of Piedmont, which is famous for its full-bodied Barolo wine. For a special occasion, use an aged Barolo if possible, otherwise a good bottle of lesser full-bodied red wine will do.

Calf's liver Venetian style

Serves 6

75g (3oz) unsalted butter
400g (14oz) onions, peeled and
  thinly sliced
125ml (4fl oz) dry white wine

800g (1¾lb) calf's liver, thinly sliced
sea salt and pepper
3 tbsp chopped flat leaf parsley, to
  serve

1 Heat half the butter in a lidded frying pan, add the onions and cook for
5 minutes or until golden. Add the wine and some salt and pepper. Cover
and braise the onions over a low heat until very tender, about 25 minutes,
stirring every now and again. Remove the onions and keep warm.
2 In the meantime, remove any gristle or membrane from the calf's liver,
then cut into strips.
3 When the onions are almost ready, melt the rest of the butter in another
frying pan. Add the liver and sauté over a high heat just until cooked
through, about 4 minutes. Add salt to taste, then mix with the braised
onions. Serve immediately, scattered with parsley.

For this classic Venetian dish, strips of calf's
liver are fried very, very quickly in butter, and
served with sweet onions braised in wine.

Steaks with pizzaiola sauce

Serves 4

50ml (2fl oz) olive oil

1 garlic clove, peeled

4 thin fillet steaks, each 150g (5oz)

400g (14oz) tomatoes, skinned, deseeded and coarsely chopped

1 tbsp chopped oregano leaves, or 2 tsp dried oregano

sea salt and pepper

To serve

few radicchio leaves, shredded (optional)

handful of rocket leaves

1 Heat the olive oil with the garlic in a heavy-based frying pan over a high heat. Add the meat and brown quickly on both sides.

2 Add the tomatoes, season with salt and pepper, and turn down the heat. Sprinkle the oregano over the meat and tomatoes, partially cover the pan and cook for 10 minutes.

3 Lift the tender pieces of meat from the pan and place on a warm plate; keep warm. Increase the heat and reduce the tomato sauce left in the pan by about half.

4 Serve the fillet steaks on a bed of shredded radicchio if you like, surrounded by the tomato sauce. Scatter a few rocket leaves on top and serve at once.

Pizzaiola sauce is so called because it features the typical pizza ingredients – olive oil, garlic, oregano and tomatoes. It is always made with fresh tomatoes, cooked briefly until softened.

Lamb braised with fennel and tomatoes

Serves 6

1 boneless shoulder of lamb, about
  1.4kg (3lb)
50ml (2fl oz) olive oil
1 onion, peeled and chopped

500g (1lb 2oz) canned peeled
  tomatoes
2 fennel bulbs, with fronds
sea salt and pepper

1 Trim the lamb of excess fat and cut into pieces, about 2cm (¾ inch) square.
Heat the olive oil in a flameproof casserole, add the chopped onion and lamb
pieces, and sauté over a medium high heat until the lamb cubes are browned
all over.

2 Add the canned tomatoes to the casserole and season with salt and pepper.
Cover and cook over a low heat for 10 minutes.

3 In the meantime, trim the fennel, reserving the feathery fronds, and cut
into slices. Add the sliced fennel to the lamb and stir well. Cook, uncovered,
for about an hour until the meat is tender, adding a little water to keep the
meat moist if necessary from time to time.

4 Taste and adjust the seasoning. Finely chop some of the reserved fennel
fronds and scatter over the braised lamb and fennel to serve.

Wild fennel grows prolifically in Sardinia, and
the rugged terrain is sheep country, so this
combination seems almost inevitable. The
flavours complement each other well, the
fennel helping to cut the richness of the lamb.

Pot roasted loin of pork

Serves 4–6

1 boned and rolled loin of pork, about 1.5kg (3¼lb)

1 celery stalk

1 onion, peeled

1 small carrot, peeled

1 garlic clove, peeled

6 sage leaves

3 rosemary sprigs

2 tbsp olive oil

150ml (¼ pint) dry white wine

3 tbsp grappa (or vodka)

2 tbsp juniper berries

250ml (8fl oz) vegetable broth (page 61)

sea salt and pepper

1 Preheat the oven to 180°C (fan oven 160°C), gas mark 4. Season the pork loin with salt and pepper all over. Very finely chop the celery, onion, carrot, garlic, sage and leaves from 1 rosemary sprig.

2 Heat the olive oil in a flameproof casserole, add the pork and brown well on all sides. Lift the pork out and set aside on a large plate.

3 Add the chopped herbs, vegetables, garlic and a little salt to the casserole and sauté for 5 minutes. Place the meat on top. Increase the heat, pour over the wine and grappa and let bubble rapidly for a minute or so, turning the meat over once. Then add the juniper and half of the broth.

4 Cover the casserole and cook in the oven for 1½ hours or until tender, turning the meat twice and adding a little more broth if the vegetables appear too dry. To impart extra flavour, lay the other 2 rosemary sprigs on top of the pork about 15 minutes before the end of cooking.

5 To serve, remove the rind from the pork, then carve into slices. Strain the cooking juices and spoon them over and around the meat.

This rather grand dish from northern Italy is perfect for a dinner party. The pork loin is pot-roasted in a sauce of wine, grappa and sage until it is meltingly tender.

Veal with pancetta and mushrooms

Serves 4

130g packet diced pancetta
4 shallots, peeled and finely chopped
6 medium flat brown mushrooms, finely diced
knob of butter

6 tbsp Marsala
handful of flat leaf parsley, finely chopped, plus extra to serve
4 veal escalopes, each about 115g (4oz)
sea salt and pepper

1 Put the pancetta dice into a large, wide sauté pan or frying pan and cook over a medium heat until the fat begins to run and the pancetta is golden at the edges. Add the shallots and cook for about 5 minutes until translucent. Add the mushrooms with the butter and cook until tender.

2 Increase the heat slightly and add half the Marsala, scraping up the sediment from the bottom of the pan with a wooden spoon. Add the parsley and seasoning. Remove with a slotted spoon; set aside.

3 Return the pan to the heat. When it is hot, add the veal escalopes with the remaining Marsala. Cook for 4 minutes on each side until tender and the liquid has evaporated. Serve topped with the pancetta and mushroom mixture, and scattered with a little chopped fresh parsley.

The rich, succulent flavour of this dish suggests that it has been cooking for hours, yet it is incredibly quick and easy to prepare.

Marinated venison stewed in red wine

Serves 6

1.4kg (3lb) boneless stewing venison
4 tbsp olive oil
2 tbsp plain flour
50g (2oz) pancetta (preferably
  smoked), diced
1 onion, peeled and chopped
½ tsp ground cinnamon
½ tsp ground cloves
284ml carton soured cream
sea salt and pepper

For the marinade

1 carrot, peeled and cut into pieces
1 onion, peeled and thickly sliced
1 celery stalk, cut into pieces
2 tbsp juniper berries, crushed
8 black peppercorns, bruised
3 cloves
1 rosemary sprig
3 tbsp olive oil
3 bay leaves
3 garlic cloves, peeled
1 bottle Barolo or other red wine

1 Put all the ingredients for the marinade into a large bowl. Cut the venison into 5cm (2 inch) pieces and add to the marinade. Stir well, then cover and leave to marinate in the refrigerator for about 12 hours.

2 Using a slotted spoon, lift the meat from the marinade, drain and pat dry with kitchen paper. Strain the marinade and reserve. Preheat the oven to 190°C (fan oven 170°C), gas mark 5.

3 Heat 2 tbsp olive oil in a large heavy-based frying pan. In batches, brown the meat all over, then transfer to a plate. Add the flour to the pan and cook until brown, stirring and scraping up the sediment on the bottom. Gradually stir in about half of the strained marinade and bring to the boil, stirring.

4 Heat the remaining 2 tbsp olive oil in a large flameproof casserole and fry the pancetta for 5 minutes. Add the onion and cook until soft.

5 Now add the meat with its juices, the wine sauce from the frying pan and about 150ml (¼ pint) of the remaining marinade. Season with salt and pepper, and add the ground spices. Bring slowly to the boil, then cover the casserole and place in the oven. Cook for about an hour or until the meat is almost tender, adding a little more of the marinade twice during cooking.

6 Add the soured cream to the casserole. Return to the oven and cook for a further 30 minutes or longer, until the meat is very tender. The cooking time will depend on the age of the animal. Serve with 'wet polenta' (see page 158).

easy
vegetables
and salads

Caponata

Serves 4

2 medium aubergines
4 tbsp olive oil
1 onion, peeled and sliced
400g can chopped tomatoes, drained
3 celery stalks, trimmed
1 tbsp capers, rinsed

50g (2oz) pitted green olives, rinsed
4 tbsp white wine vinegar
1 tbsp caster sugar
2 tbsp pine nuts
handful of flat leaf parsley, chopped
sea salt and pepper

1 Cut the aubergines into 2.5cm (1 inch) cubes. Sprinkle with salt, place in a colander, cover and weight down. Set aside to degorge the bitter juices for 15 minutes, then rinse to remove the salt and pat dry with kitchen paper.

2 Heat 3 tbsp of the olive oil in a large frying pan. Add the aubergine cubes and fry, turning, until brown and tender. Drain on kitchen paper, and keep to one side.

3 Heat the remaining 1 tbsp olive oil in a saucepan, add the onion and fry for 5 minutes until golden. Add the tomatoes and some salt and pepper, and simmer for 15 minutes.

4 Meanwhile, cut the celery into 1cm (½ inch) pieces. Add to the tomato sauce with the capers, olives, wine vinegar and sugar. Simmer for a further 15 minutes until reduced slightly, stirring occasionally.

5 Put the aubergine and pine nuts into a serving dish and pour over the tomato sauce. Stir, then leave to stand for at least 30 minutes. Scatter with the chopped parsley just before serving.

A classic sweet-sour Sicilian, which can be served hot or cold, as an antipasto or vegetable dish. It keeps well in the fridge for a few days.

Tuscan cabbage and cannellini beans

Serves 6

200g (7oz) dried white cannellini
  beans, soaked in cold water
  overnight
2 rosemary sprigs
3 bay leaves
3 thyme sprigs
3 flat leaf parsley sprigs

4 garlic cloves, unpeeled
450g (1lb) cavolo nero (or green
  cabbage), stalks removed
6 slightly dry slices of fine-textured,
  country-style bread
extra virgin olive oil, to drizzle
sea salt and pepper

1 Drain the cannellini beans and place in a large pan. Add plenty of cold
water to cover, the herbs and 3 unpeeled garlic cloves. Bring to the boil, then
reduce the heat and cook for about 1½ hours or until the beans are tender.
2 Preheat the oven to 200°C (fan oven 180°C), gas mark 6. Roughly chop the
cavolo nero leaves and add to a pan of boiling salted water. Return to the boil
and simmer for 10–15 minutes until tender.
3 Arrange the bread slices in a single layer on a baking sheet and bake in
the oven for 3 minutes. Turn them over and bake for a further 3 minutes. In
the meantime, peel and halve the remaining garlic clove. While the bread is
hot, rub one side with the garlic.
4 Drain the beans and discard the herbs and garlic. Arrange the bread on a
plate, garlic-side up. Scoop the cavolo nero from the pan using a slotted
spoon, drain well and arrange on the bread slices. Spoon the hot cannellini
beans on top. Drizzle with extra virgin olive oil, season with salt and pepper
and serve immediately.

This can be served as a starter or antipasto, or
as a vegetable. If you haven't time to cook
dried beans, use a 400g can cannellini beans
instead: drain, rinse and flavour with a little
crushed garlic and chopped thyme.

Marinated courgettes

Illustrated on previous pages

Serves 6

9 large courgettes, trimmed

175ml (6fl oz) olive oil

For the dressing

large handful of mint leaves,
  coarsely chopped

3 garlic cloves, peeled and finely
  chopped

6 tbsp white wine vinegar

4 tbsp extra virgin olive oil

sea salt

1 Preheat the oven to 140°C (fan oven 120°C), gas mark 1, and line two large baking trays with baking parchment.

2 Cut the courgettes lengthways into thin slices and place in a single layer on the lined trays. Leave in the oven for about an hour to dry out completely without colouring.

3 Heat the olive oil in a large frying pan and fry the courgettes in batches until golden; there's no need to turn them. Drain carefully on kitchen paper.

4 Transfer the courgette slices to a serving bowl and sprinkle with the chopped mint and garlic. Drizzle over the wine vinegar and extra virgin olive oil, and season with salt to taste. Cover and leave to stand for 2 hours before serving or, better still, overnight.

This is a typical recipe from Campania. Finely sliced courgettes are oven-dried, then fried and marinated in wine vinegar and fruity olive oil with fresh mint. For optimum flavour, marinate the courgettes overnight.

Peas with spring onions and pancetta

Serves 4–6

2 tbsp olive oil

2 bunches of spring onions, trimmed
and roughly chopped

150g (5oz) pancetta, diced

500g (1lb 2oz) podded fresh or
frozen peas (preferably fresh)

handful of flat leaf parsley, chopped,
plus a sprig to serve

sea salt and pepper

1 Heat the olive oil in a large frying pan over a medium heat. Add the spring onions and pancetta and sauté until the onions are translucent.

2 Add the peas, salt, pepper and 125ml (4fl oz) boiling water. Bring to a simmer and cook uncovered until the peas are tender, about 5–7 minutes for fresh peas, 3–4 minutes for frozen ones.

3 Drain the peas and toss with the chopped parsley. Transfer to a warm bowl and top with the parsley sprig to serve.

Freshly podded young peas are cooked together quickly with sautéed spring onions and chopped salty Italian bacon in one pan.

Baked onions stuffed with prosciutto

Serves 4 or 8

8 large white onions, peeled

2 tbsp coarse white breadcrumbs

½ tbsp milk

150g (5oz) prosciutto, finely chopped

6 tbsp freshly grated Parmesan
   cheese

1 medium egg, beaten

15g (½oz) unsalted butter, in pieces,
   plus extra to grease

sea salt and pepper

1 Add the white onions to a pan of boiling salted water and simmer for
15 minutes. Meanwhile, soak the breadcrumbs in the milk. Preheat the oven
to 180°C (fan oven 160°C), gas mark 4.

2 Drain the onions, reserving the liquid. Rinse under cold running water,
then drain and pat dry with kitchen paper. Cut a thin slice from the top of
each onion and scoop out the centres, using a teaspoon; keep half of the
onion flesh that you remove. Place the onion 'cups' upside down on a board
while you prepare the filling.

3 Finely chop the reserved onion. Squeeze the breadcrumbs to remove excess
liquid and place in a bowl with the onion. Add the prosciutto, Parmesan and
beaten egg. Season with salt and pepper and mix well. Spoon the stuffing
into the onion shells.

4 Grease a baking dish with butter and arrange the onions in it. Dot with
butter and moisten the onions with 50ml (2fl oz) of the reserved cooking
liquid. Bake for 40 minutes, basting the onions from time to time with the
pan juices. Serve hot.

Delicious onions, stuffed with breadcrumbs
flavoured with prosciutto and Parmesan, then
baked until sweet and tender. Serve as an
antipasto, or as a vegetable side dish.

Cabbage parcels with leeks and mushrooms

Illustrated on previous pages

Serves 4

1 Savoy cabbage

225g (8oz) leeks, washed and trimmed

125g (4oz) flat field mushrooms, wiped

25g (1oz) unsalted butter

2 garlic cloves, peeled and finely chopped

50g (2oz) slivered almonds

2–3 tsp lemon juice

2 tsp paprika

1 medium egg, beaten

150ml (¼ pint) vegetable broth (page 61)

sea salt and pepper

1 Preheat the oven to 200°C (fan oven 180°C), gas mark 6. Select 8 large, darker outer leaves from the cabbage. Blanch these leaves in boiling salted water, or steam, for 1–2 minutes to soften slightly. Cut away the tough centre stalks.

2 Finely chop the leeks, mushrooms and 225g (8oz) of the remaining cabbage. Melt the butter in a large frying pan. Add the garlic, leeks, mushrooms and chopped cabbage and fry gently, stirring frequently, for 10 minutes.

3 Add the almonds, lemon juice and paprika to the leek mixture and cook over a low heat for 5 minutes. Remove from the heat and allow to cool. Add the beaten egg and some salt and pepper to the cooled stuffing and mix well.

4 Divide the stuffing between the blanched cabbage leaves and roll up tightly, tucking in the sides as you roll. Pack the cabbage parcels into an ovenproof dish, placing them join-side down. Pour the vegetable broth around them and cover the dish with foil. Bake in the oven for 20 minutes. Serve hot.

Stuffed vegetables are commonplace in Italy, and most recipes come from around Rome. Here, though, the aspect is more northern, in that cabbage is used. These parcels can be assembled ahead, and the filling can be varied – try mozzarella and anchovies, for instance.

Roman artichokes

Illustrated on previous pages

Serves 4
4 medium artichokes
1 lemon, cut in half
3 bay leaves
150ml (¼ pint) dry white wine

For the dressing
large handful of mint leaves
2 garlic cloves, peeled
3–4 tbsp extra virgin olive oil
2 tbsp white wine vinegar
sea salt and pepper

1 Prepare the artichokes one at a time. Trim the base of the stalk at an angle, then peel the stem. Cut off the leaves about 5mm (¼ inch) from the top. Rub the cut surfaces with a lemon half. Now start peeling away the artichoke leaves, removing at least 4 layers, until you reach the pale leaves. Spread the top leaves and reach down with a teaspoon to scrape out the choke. Immerse the artichoke in a bowl of cold water with the other lemon half added (to prevent discoloration). Repeat with the rest of the artichokes.
2 Place the bay leaves, lemon halves, wine and artichokes in a large pan and add enough cold water to cover. (The artichokes should fit snugly in the pan.) Bring to the boil, cover and simmer for about 30–35 minutes until the artichokes are tender. Drain thoroughly.
3 To make the dressing, chop the mint leaves very finely together with the garlic, then place in a bowl with the olive oil, wine vinegar and salt and pepper to taste. Whisk to blend thoroughly.
4 Arrange the artichokes upside down (with their stalks sticking up) on serving plates. While still warm, pour over the dressing and serve.

Artichokes grow all over Italy, but Rome is especially renowned for its small, tender artichokes. Try to buy young artichokes with long stalks, as these are tender and won't yet have developed much of a choke.

Neapolitan vegetable casserole

Serves 4

1 medium aubergine
1 medium onion, peeled
1 red pepper
2 medium potatoes, peeled
1 courgette, trimmed
3 tbsp olive oil

1 garlic clove, peeled and crushed
2–3 tsp fennel seeds, crushed
400g can peeled plum tomatoes
6 tbsp red wine
2 tsp dried oregano
sea salt and pepper

1 Cut the aubergine into cubes. Sprinkle with salt, place in a colander, cover and weight down. Leave to degorge the bitter juices for 15 minutes.
2 Meanwhile, chop the onion. Halve, core and deseed the red pepper. Cut the red pepper, potatoes and courgette into similar sized chunks. Rinse the aubergine cubes and pat dry.
3 Heat the olive oil in a saucepan, add the onion and cook gently for about 5 minutes or until softened, then add the garlic and cook for a minute. Add all the vegetables and remaining ingredients. Bring to a simmer and cook gently for 25–30 minutes until the vegetables are tender, adding a little water to moisten during cooking if necessary. Serve hot.

This is Naples' answer to ratatouille. It's an easy dish, and one that can be cooked ahead of time. Vary the vegetables as you like – try adding celery or fennel.

Creamy potato bake with prosciutto

Serves 6

1kg (2¼lb) old potatoes (such as
  Maris Piper, King Edward,
  Pentland Crown)
25g (1oz) unsalted butter
125g (4oz) prosciutto slices

450ml (¾ pint) milk
250ml (8fl oz) single cream
225g (8oz) Parmesan cheese,
  freshly grated
freshly grated nutmeg, to taste
sea salt and pepper

1 Preheat the oven to 180°C (fan oven 160°C), gas mark 4. Peel the potatoes and slice them thinly. Grease a large shallow baking dish with half of the butter. Lay the potato slices in the dish, overlapping them slightly. Lay the slices of prosciutto on top.

2 In a bowl, mix together the milk, cream and half of the grated Parmesan, and season with nutmeg, salt and pepper. Pour the mixture over the potatoes. Sprinkle with the remaining Parmesan and dot with the rest of the butter.

3 Bake in the oven until the potatoes are tender, about 45 minutes. If necessary, increase the oven temperature towards the end of the baking time to brown the crust. Serve hot.

Similar to the French gratin dauphinoise, this is ideal served after (or with) a meat dish. A little finely chopped garlic can be added, or for a more subtle taste, rub a cut garlic clove around the dish with the butter. The casserole can be cooked ahead and reheated to serve.

Braised fennel with pecorino

Serves 4
2 fennel bulbs, with fronds
25g (1oz) unsalted butter
1 tbsp olive oil

sea salt and pepper
150g (5oz) pecorino cheese, pared
   into shavings, to serve

1 Trim the fennel bulbs, reserving a few of the feathery fronds for the garnish. Cut each fennel bulb in half from top to bottom and blanch in boiling salted water for 5 minutes, then drain.
2 Melt the butter with the olive oil in a heavy-based sauté pan or frying pan over a medium heat. Add the halved fennel bulbs and cook for 10–12 minutes or until tender and golden brown, turning from time to time to colour evenly. Season with salt and pepper.
3 Transfer to a warm serving plate and scatter with pecorino shavings. Garnish with the fennel fronds and serve at once.

Fennel is sautéed in butter and olive oil until tender, then served topped with pecorino cheese shavings. This tempting dish is especially good after fish.

Classic Italian salad

Serves 4
3 baby Cos or Little Gem lettuce
For the dressing
finely grated zest and juice of
   1 lemon
½ garlic clove, peeled and crushed
4 tbsp extra virgin olive oil
1 tbsp freshly grated Parmesan
   cheese
sea salt and pepper

1 Separate the lettuce leaves, wash and dry well, then place in a salad bowl.
2 To make the dressing, whisk the lemon zest and juice, crushed garlic and extra virgin olive oil together in a bowl to combine, seasoning with salt and pepper to taste. Add the freshly grated Parmesan, which will instantly make the dressing thicker and creamier. Use at once, or whiz in a blender or food processor for a smoother dressing.
3 Toss the leaves in the dressing and serve, as a side salad – either with or after the main course.

Italians love their salads and many fine leaves originate from Italy, including peppery rocket, lollo rosso, lollo biondo and radicchio. This dressing – my all-time favourite – is suited to sturdier leaves, such as Cos, and bitter leaves like frisée.

Peppery leaf salad in an anchovy dressing

Serves 4

300g (11oz) mixed rocket, spinach, lollo rosso, radicchio and frisée (or any combination of these leaves)

For the dressing

125ml (4fl oz) fruity extra virgin olive oil

1 shallot, peeled and finely chopped

6 anchovy fillets in oil, drained and chopped

1 garlic clove, peeled and finely chopped

175ml (6fl oz) dry white wine

handful of basil leaves, torn

sea salt and pepper

1 Wash the salad leaves and dry well, then place in a salad bowl.

2 To make the dressing, gently heat the extra virgin olive oil in a small pan, then add the shallot and sweat until soft. Add the chopped anchovies, garlic, wine and basil leaves. Gently warm through, then whiz in a blender or food processor until smooth. Pass the dressing through a fine sieve and season to taste (but go easy with the salt).

3 Pour the dressing over the salad, toss gently and serve, as a side salad – either with or after the main course.

Very fresh salad leaves are essential for a true Italian salad. Wash them just before assembling the salad and carefully pat dry with kitchen paper.

Salad leaves in a balsamic vinaigrette

Serves 4

300g (11oz) mixed rocket, Little Gem
lettuce, lamb's lettuce, radicchio
and frisée (or any combination of
these leaves)

For the dressing

2 tbsp good, aged balsamic vinegar
4 tbsp extra virgin olive oil
4 tbsp sunflower oil
sea salt and pepper

1 Wash the salad leaves and dry well, then place in a salad bowl.
2 To make the dressing, in a bowl, whisk the balsamic vinegar with the extra
virgin olive oil and sunflower oil until emulsified, and season with salt and
pepper to taste.
3 Pour the dressing over the salad, toss to mix and serve, as a side salad –
either with or after the main course.

This vinaigrette is suitable for dressing meat
and vegetables, as well as salad leaves.
Balsamic jelly can be used in place of the
vinegar – simply dilute it to taste with oil to
make your dressing as thick as you like.

Pecorino and fennel salad

Serves 4
2 small fennel bulbs, trimmed
handful of rocket leaves
250g (9oz) pecorino cheese

40g (1½oz) pine nuts, toasted
squeeze of lemon juice
3 tbsp extra virgin olive oil
sea salt and pepper

1 Cut the fennel into very thin slices and arrange on individual plates with the rocket leaves. Using a swivel vegetable peeler, shave the pecorino cheese into wafer-thin slices and scatter over the fennel and rocket.
2 Sprinkle with the toasted pine nuts, add a squeeze of lemon juice and drizzle with the extra virgin olive oil. Season with salt and pepper and serve.

In Italy, this salad is usually eaten after the main course as a digestive, but it can also be served as a starter.

Sicilian fennel and orange salad

Serves 4

6 oranges (use blood oranges when in season)

1 fennel bulb, trimmed

3 tbsp chopped fresh walnuts

2 tbsp extra virgin olive oil

1 small Cos lettuce, separated into leaves

sea salt and pepper

1 Peel the oranges, removing all white pith, and then slice horizontally into thin rounds.

2 Slice the fennel bulb thinly, reserving a few of the feathery fronds for garnish. Snip the fennel fronds into small pieces.

3 Combine the fennel and oranges, snipped fennel fronds and walnuts in a large shallow bowl. Dress with the extra virgin olive oil, season with salt and pepper, and leave to stand for an hour or so to let the flavours infuse, turning occasionally.

4 Serve the salad in individual bowls, adding a few Cos leaves to each bowl.

This refreshing southern salad – dressed with fruity olive oil – is best served as a side salad, either with grilled or barbecued meat or fish, or to follow the main course.

easy
desserts
and sweets

Meringues with chocolate sauce

Serves 4
3 egg whites
175g (6oz) caster sugar
250ml (8fl oz) double cream

For the chocolate sauce
200g (7oz) luxury dark chocolate,
  broken into pieces
125ml (4fl oz) milk

1 Preheat the oven to its lowest setting, 110°C (fan oven 100°C), gas mark ¼. Line a large baking sheet with baking parchment.

2 Whisk the egg whites in a clean bowl until stiff and glossy. With patience, add the sugar very gradually, whisking well between each addition. The meringue should be stiff and shiny.

3 Spoon the meringue into a piping bag fitted with a 2.5cm (1 inch) plain tip and pipe about 16 mounds, about 5cm (2 inches) in diameter, on the baking sheet, spacing them well apart.

4 Bake the meringues in the oven for about 2 hours until crisp and dry, but still white. Peel the meringues away from the paper and place on a wire rack. Leave to cool completely.

5 For the sauce, melt the chocolate with the milk in a heatproof bowl set over a pan of gently simmering water. Take off the heat and stir until smooth. Allow to cool slightly, or completely if you prefer to serve the sauce at room temperature.

6 To assemble, whip the cream until it holds soft peaks. Sandwich the cold meringues together in pairs with the cream, then arrange on a serving dish. Pour the warm or cool chocolate sauce over the meringues and serve.

Grilled fruit salad with zabaglione sauce

Illustrated on previous pages

Serves 4
100g (3½oz) strawberries, hulled
1 kiwi fruit
1 pear
100g (3½oz) raspberries
2 tbsp Vin Santo (or 1 tbsp
   Marsala)

For the zabaglione
3 egg yolks
75g (3oz) caster sugar
2½ tbsp Marsala
To finish
1–2 tsp icing sugar, sifted, to
   sprinkle

1 Halve or slice the strawberries. Peel and slice the kiwi fruit. Peel, core and slice the pear. Leave the raspberries whole. Combine the fruit in a shallow baking dish (or individual grillproof dishes) and sprinkle with the Vin Santo or Marsala.

2 To make the zabaglione, put the egg yolks and caster sugar into a heatproof bowl and whisk until creamy and almost white in colour. Gradually add the Marsala, whisking constantly until the mixture is well combined.

3 Place the bowl over a saucepan of simmering water and cook over a medium heat, beating constantly with the whisk, until the zabaglione is creamy and thick.

4 Pour the hot zabaglione over the fruit. Sprinkle with icing sugar. Place under a preheated hot grill for 30 seconds, or wave a blow-torch over the surface until the zabaglione begins to brown. Serve immediately, with vanilla ice cream if you wish.

Fresh seasonal fruits – especially peaches, nectarines, cherries and pears – are often served at the end of a meal in Italy. As an alternative, I sometimes serve a medley of fruits under a caramelised zabaglione topping. Either use a large shallow baking dish or individual gratin dishes.

Baked stuffed peaches

Illustrated on previous pages

Serves 4

4 large ripe peaches

9 amaretti biscuits, crushed

25g (1oz) ground almonds

1 egg yolk

1 tbsp cocoa powder, sifted

300ml (½ pint) dry white wine

2 tbsp soft brown sugar

1 Preheat the oven to 180°C (fan oven 160°C), gas mark 4. Wash the peaches and pat dry. Cut them in half following the natural line and remove the stone. Using a teaspoon, scoop out a little of the pulp from the middle of each peach half to create a cavity. Finely chop the scooped-out pulp.

2 In a bowl, combine the chopped peach pulp, crushed amaretti biscuits, ground almonds, egg yolk and cocoa powder, and mix thoroughly until evenly blended. (Alternatively, whiz in a food processor for a few seconds until smooth.)

3 Fill the peach cavities with the almond mixture and place side by side in a baking dish. Pour the wine over the peaches, sprinkle with the brown sugar and bake in the oven for 25 minutes.

4 Allow the peaches to cool and serve at room temperature, drizzled with the cooking juices.

Italian peaches are prized for their juicy, fragrant flesh. This recipe is a classic from Lombardy. Halved peaches are stuffed with a mixture of ground almonds, crumbled amaretti and cocoa powder, then drizzled with dry white wine and baked until tender.

Ricotta cheesecake with strawberry sauce

Illustrated on previous pages

Serves 6

For the pastry

275g (10oz) Italian '00' flour, plus
   extra to dust
50g (2oz) caster sugar
125g (4oz) unsalted butter, softened
1 egg, plus 1 egg yolk
½ tsp vanilla extract
finely grated zest of 1 small
   unwaxed lemon
½ tsp baking powder

For the filling

2 eggs, separated
125g (4oz) granulated sugar
50g (2oz) unsalted butter, softened
finely grated zest of 1 unwaxed lemon
1 tsp vanilla extract
275g (10oz) ricotta cheese
1 tsp thin honey
1 tsp baking powder

For the sauce

150g (5oz) strawberries, hulled
juice of 1 lemon
1 tbsp caster sugar

1 To make the pastry, combine all the ingredients in a food processor and process until the mixture is evenly blended and comes together as a ball of dough. If the pastry is a little too sticky, add a bit more flour. Wrap the dough in cling film and leave to rest in the refrigerator for about 30 minutes.

2 Preheat the oven to 150°C (fan oven 130°C), gas mark 2. Roll out the pastry on a lightly floured surface to a 3mm (⅛ inch) thickness and use to line a 20cm (8 inch) springform tin, or deep loose-based flan tin, pressing the pastry on to the bottom and up the sides. Set aside.

3 For the filling, beat the egg yolks, sugar, butter, lemon zest and vanilla together with an electric mixer until smooth. Add the ricotta, honey and baking powder and mix gently until evenly blended. In a separate bowl, whisk the egg whites until they hold firm peaks, then gently fold into the filling.

4 Pour the filling into the pastry case and bake in the oven for 2½ hours. Leave to cool in the tin on a wire rack. Chill until ready to serve.

5 For the sauce, purée the strawberries, lemon juice and sugar in a blender, then pass through a sieve into a bowl. Cover and chill for 30 minutes.

6 Carefully unmould the cheesecake on to a flat plate. Serve in slices, topped with a ladleful of strawberry sauce.

Almond pudding with bitter chocolate sauce

Serves 4
200g (7oz) blanched almonds
grated zest of 1 unwaxed lemon
2 tsp powdered gelatine
375ml (13fl oz) milk

125g (4oz) caster sugar
1 tsp vanilla extract
1 tbsp Grand Marnier
125g (4oz) luxury dark, bitter
   chocolate, finely chopped

1 Put the blanched almonds into a blender or food processor and grind to a fine paste. Transfer to a bowl and stir in 175ml (6fl oz) warm water and the lemon zest. Mix thoroughly and set aside to rest for 1 hour. Strain the almond liquid through a sieve into a bowl.

2 Sprinkle the gelatine over 1 tbsp cold water in a bowl and leave to soften for 5 minutes. Pour 150ml (¼ pint) of the milk into a saucepan and add the sugar and vanilla extract. Slowly bring to the boil over a low heat, stirring to dissolve the sugar. Add the gelatine and whisk briefly to dissolve.

3 Remove from the heat and add the almond liquid, Grand Marnier and remaining milk. Mix well, then pour into a 25cm (10 inch) ring mould or 1 litre (1¾ pint) pudding basin and refrigerate for 3 hours.

4 Melt the chocolate in a bowl set over a pan of hot water. Stir until melted and very smooth. Remove the bowl from the pan and allow to cool slightly.

5 Briefly dip the mould into hot water, then turn out the pudding on to a serving plate. Drizzle some of the melted chocolate sauce on top; hand the rest separately.

This is a very old recipe, dating back to the Middle Ages, featuring almonds. These were introduced by the Arabs into Sicily during their occupation of southern Italy. A dark chocolate sauce complements the flavour well.

My grandmother's espresso pudding

Serves 4

450ml (¾ pint) brewed espresso
   coffee, cooled
150g (5oz) caster sugar

5 large eggs, beaten
1 tsp lemon juice
350ml (12fl oz) double cream

1 Combine the cooled espresso and half the sugar in a large bowl and stir well. Add the beaten eggs, a little at a time, mixing thoroughly.

2 Put the remaining sugar, the lemon juice and 1 tbsp water into a small heavy-based pan. Cook over a medium to high heat until the mixture turns a pale caramel colour. Immediately pour the caramel into a shallow 25cm (10 inch) ring mould or 1 litre (1¾ pint) shallow round baking dish, tilting it in all directions to distribute the caramel over the bottom and sides. Continue to tilt until the caramel has hardened. Leave to cool for 30 minutes.

3 Preheat the oven to 180°C (fan oven 160°C), gas mark 4. Pour the coffee mixture into the caramel-lined mould and place in a large roasting tin containing enough water to come halfway up the sides of the mould. Bake in the oven for 1 hour until the pudding is set and a toothpick or wooden cocktail stick inserted in the centre comes out dry. Allow the pudding to cool for 1 hour.

4 To serve, unmould on to a serving plate. Whip the cream until thick and pile into the centre (if you have used a ring mould), or serve individual portions with a dollop of whipped cream.

Apple cake

Illustrated on previous pages

Serves 6–8

1–2 tsp vegetable oil
1–2 tbsp dried breadcrumbs
125g (4oz) unsalted butter
500g (1lb 2oz) Golden Delicious apples
4 eggs
150g (5oz) caster sugar
150g (5oz) Italian '00' flour
1 tsp baking powder
pinch of salt
6 tbsp milk
finely grated zest of 2 unwaxed
  lemons
icing sugar, sifted, to dust
rosemary sprigs, to finish (optional)

1 Preheat the oven to 180°C (fan oven 160°C), gas mark 4. Brush the inside of a 23cm (9 inch) cake tin with the oil, then sprinkle with the breadcrumbs and shake off the excess. Melt the butter and set aside to cool. Peel, quarter and core the apples, then slice thinly.

2 Put the eggs and sugar into a heatproof bowl over a pan of gently simmering water. Whisk for 10–15 minutes until the mixture is thick and pale, and leaves a trail when the beaters are lifted. Remove the bowl from the heat and continue whisking until the mixture is cool.

3 Sift the flour with the baking powder and salt. Fold half of this mixture gently into the whisked eggs and sugar. Slowly trickle the melted butter around the edge of the bowl and fold it in gently. Take care to avoid knocking out the air and losing volume. Fold in the remaining flour mixture, then the milk and lemon zest, and finally the apple slices.

4 Pour the mixture into the prepared tin. Bake for 45 minutes or until a skewer inserted in the centre comes out clean. Leave in the tin for 5 minutes, then turn out on to a wire rack and leave to cool. To serve, dust the top of the cake liberally with icing sugar and scatter with rosemary sprigs if liked.

This light Genoese sponge layered with apples is delicious with coffee for breakfast, or for an afternoon snack. To vary the flavour, try adding a little finely chopped fresh rosemary to the mixture.

Chocolate salami

Serves 4–6

90g (3¼oz) raisins
225g (8oz) luxury dark chocolate
50g (2oz) unsalted butter
50g (2oz) caster sugar
90g (3¼oz) blanched whole almonds,
 coarsely chopped
225g (8oz) Petit Beurre type biscuits,
 coarsely crushed
1 tbsp brandy
50g (2oz) whole mixed candied peel,
 coarsely chopped
1 egg yolk

1 Soak the raisins in warm water to cover for about 15 minutes until plump, then drain and set aside.
2 Break the chocolate into pieces and place in a large heatproof bowl with the butter. Place over a saucepan of gently simmering water until melted. Remove the bowl from the pan and stir until smooth.
3 Add the sugar, almonds, biscuits, raisins, brandy and candied peel to the melted chocolate and mix well. Return the bowl to the pan, add the egg yolk and stir until evenly incorporated. Take the bowl off the pan and leave the mixture to cool completely.
4 Turn the mixture on to a sheet of baking parchment and shape into a roll with your hands. Wrap the 'chocolate salami' in the paper and twist the ends to seal. Refrigerate for several hours to firm up. To serve, remove the paper, cut the salami into thin slices and arrange on a serving plate.

This sweet from Emilia-Romagna is a mixture of chocolate, nuts, biscuits and brandy, rolled into a sausage, chilled to set and then sliced. You can make the rolls as fat or thin as you like, but be warned – the mixture is very rich! Small discs make ideal petits fours to serve with coffee.

Almond biscuits

Serves 4–6

275g (10oz) Italian '00' flour
175g (6oz) caster sugar
1½ tsp baking powder
½ tsp salt
2 eggs, plus 1 egg yolk
125g (4oz) blanched whole almonds,
    roughly chopped

1 Preheat the oven to 180°C (fan oven 160°C), gas mark 4. Mix the flour, sugar, baking powder and salt together in a bowl. Add the eggs and egg yolk, and mix well to form a smooth dough. Knead in the chopped almonds.
2 Divide the dough into 4 portions and form each into a cigar-shaped log. Place the logs on a floured baking sheet, spacing them well apart. Bake for about 20 minutes until golden brown.
3 Cut the logs into 1cm (½ inch) slices while still warm. Separate them and lay on the baking sheet. Bake for another 15 minutes.
4 Transfer the biscuits to a wire rack to cool. Store in an airtight container until required.

Almonds are used as a basis for these crisp Tuscan biscuits, which are traditionally served with Vin Santo. You can vary the recipe if you like, adding hazelnuts instead of the almonds, or some chopped chocolate.

Chocolate coated figs with almond stuffing

Makes 12
12 whole blanched almonds
finely pared zest of 3 oranges

12 dried figs, preferably Italian
225g (8oz) luxury dark chocolate

1 Preheat the grill to medium. Spread the almonds on a foil-lined grill pan and toast under the grill until golden, turning frequently and watching carefully to make sure they don't burn. Allow to cool.
2 Chop the orange zest very finely and scatter on a board. Slit the figs vertically and place an almond inside each one. Roll the figs in the orange zest to coat all over.
3 Meanwhile, break the chocolate into pieces and put in a heatproof bowl set over a saucepan of simmering water. Leave until melted, then take off the heat and stir until smooth.
4 One at a time, spear the figs with a fork and partially dip in the chocolate, turning to coat all round. Place the figs on a sheet of baking parchment and leave to dry.

This dried fig delicacy comes from Calabria. The attractive chocolate-dipped figs make an ideal foodie gift, especially at Christmas. Use good quality dried figs.

Italian cheese, grapes and balsamic jelly

Illustrated on previous pages

Serves 4
generous wedge of pecorino or
   Gorgonzola cheese
jar of balsamic jelly
bunch of black or green grapes

1 Bring the cheese to room temperature well in advance of the meal.
2 Serve a wedge of either cheese with a generous spoonful of balsamic jelly, and grapes. Balsamic jelly tastes wonderful and is the ideal complement to full flavoured Gorgonzola or a sharp pecorino.

In Italy, cheese is eaten as a course on its own, often instead of a dessert. Typically a generous wedge of one superb cheese is accompanied by fruit such as grapes, apples or pears, or nuts, or some crisp celery or fennel. Of course, you can serve a selection of cheeses if you prefer.

Sardinian cheese biscuits

Serves 4

150g (5oz) semolina or Italian '00' flour

1 small egg, beaten

75g (3oz) pecorino cheese, freshly grated

pinch of salt

olive oil, for deep-frying

1 Pile the semolina or flour into a mound on a work surface and make a well in the middle. Add the egg, grated pecorino and salt. Mix the ingredients in the well together and gradually incorporate the flour, adding enough water (about 4 tbsp) to make a soft dough.

2 Break off small pieces of the dough, roll into balls, then flatten to make very thin discs.

3 Heat the olive oil in a deep-fat fryer or deep heavy-based saucepan to 190°C, or until a cube of bread dropped in browns in 30 seconds. Deep-fry the dough rounds, a few at a time, for about 5–6 minutes until golden. Drain well on kitchen paper and cool on a wire rack.

Make these savoury biscuits to serve at the end of a meal with Italian cheese and fruit. Alternatively, you can serve them with drinks.

Gorgonzola, pear and toasted walnuts

Serves 4
12–16 fresh walnuts
4 ripe pears
125g (4oz) Gorgonzola cheese
thin honey (preferably fragrant)
    to drizzle

1 Preheat the oven to 200°C (fan oven 180°C), gas mark 6. Scatter the walnuts on a baking tray and toast in the oven for 5–7 minutes; don't let them burn.
2 Peel, quarter and core the pears, and then cut into thin wedges. Arrange the pear wedges on individual plates, scatter over the toasted walnuts and crumble the cheese on top of the pears.
3 Drizzle over a little honey and eat with a knife and fork.

An unusual Italian custom is to round off a meal with a combination of cheese, fruit and nuts, drizzled with a little fragrant honey. The contrast of saltiness and sweetness is wonderful. Pecorino works equally well here.

Index